Learning eBPF

eBPF

*High performance observability, networking,
and security programming on Linux*

Michael Kehoe

www.bpbonline.com

First Edition 2025

Copyright © BPB Publications, India

ISBN: 978-93-65898-859

To View Complete
BPB Publications Catalogue
Scan the QR Code:

Dedicated to

My Mum, Dad, and brother for their
unwavering love, support, and belief in me

About the Author

Michael Kehoe is a distinguished author, speaker, and senior staff cloud and reliability architect at Confluent. In his current role, he is spearheading a comprehensive initiative to revamp the company's cloud platform.

Previously, as a senior staff **site reliability engineer** (**SRE**) at LinkedIn, Michael played a pivotal role in orchestrating LinkedIn's seamless transition to the Microsoft Azure platform. His expertise in reliability engineering was instrumental in ensuring the platform's stability and performance. During his tenure at LinkedIn, Michael led critical initiatives in incident response, disaster recovery, visibility engineering, and reliability principles. He was also embedded with the profile, traffic, and espresso (KV Store) teams. Having successfully overseen the construction of LinkedIn's final physical data center, Michael assumed a pivotal role in shaping the infrastructure blueprint for LinkedIn's expansion into Microsoft Azure.

About the Reviewers

❖ **Yusheng Zheng** is a software engineer, researcher, and open-source advocate with a strong passion for eBPF and **large language models** (**LLMs**). As the creator of the eunomia-bpf project, Yusheng has been actively involved in advancing lightweight eBPF development frameworks, exploring their potential beyond Linux and integrating them with emerging technologies. She has spoken at major conferences, including KubeCon, eBPF Summit, and the Linux Plumbers Conference. When not immersed in code, she shares her insights and learnings on her blogs and enjoys collaborating on innovative projects with fellow developers and researchers.

❖ **Hudson Coutinho:** Working as a DevOps engineer since 2018, he has participated in strategic projects for large national and international companies, dedicating myself to building and improving robust and scalable DevOps architectures.

Throughout their career, they have executed several migrations to the cloud, created environments in Kubernetes, created micro-services in Docker, implemented complete CI/CD pipelines, and optimized internal processes, always with a keen eye for efficiency and security.

As head of DevOps, Hudson has led DevOps teams and multidisciplinary teams, guiding them to achieve results that are always based on agile principles and focused on automation, seeking continuous improvement.

Acknowledgement

First and foremost, I extend my heartfelt appreciation to my family and friends for their unwavering support and encouragement throughout this journey. Their love and encouragement have been a constant source of motivation.

I am immensely grateful to BPB Publications and the team for their guidance and expertise in bringing this book to fruition. Their support and assistance were invaluable in navigating the complexities of the publishing process.

I would also like to acknowledge the reviewers, technical experts, and editors who provided valuable feedback and contributed to the refinement of this manuscript. Their insights and suggestions have significantly enhanced the quality of the book.

Last but not least, I want to express our gratitude to the readers who have shown interest in this book. Your support and encouragement have been deeply appreciated.

Thank you to everyone who has played a part in making this book a reality.

Preface

In today's complex computing environment, having a deep understanding of system behavior is a necessity. Maintaining performance, efficiency, security, and reliability, demands deep insights into the inner workings of our infrastructure. Traditional monitoring and debugging tools, while useful, are often unhelpful when faced with the scale and intricacy of modern systems. These tools often operate at a high level, providing aggregate metrics that do not provide information about individual processes, network interactions, or kernel events. They can also introduce significant overhead, impacting the very systems they are supposed to observe. This is where **extended Berkeley Packet Filter (eBPF)** fills these gaps, offering a revolutionary approach to system observability.

eBPF is the evolution of the **classic Berkeley Packet Filter (cBPF)** which was originally created in the 1990's. It allows for user-defined, sandboxed bytecode to be executed by the kernel. eBPF represents a paradigm shift in how we can interact with and use the kernel, opening up unprecedented possibilities for innovation in areas such as observability, networking, and security. This book will move beyond theoretical concepts and demonstrate the practical applications of eBPF, providing concrete examples of how to leverage eBPF for a wide range of applications.

Divided into ten chapters, this book provides a complete guide to the eBPF ecosystem. We start by exploring the foundations of classic BPF, understanding its history, and examining its core architecture. From there, we observe the evolution of eBPF, detailing its history, features, and the key advancements that distinguish it from its predecessor.

Chapter 3 provides a deep dive into eBPF programming concepts, covering essential elements such as the bpf() system call, program types, attach types, maps, and helper functions. Chapter 4 then explores the diverse array of libraries and frameworks available for eBPF development, ranging from libbpf and BCC to language-specific options like ebpf-go and Aya.

Chapter 5 guides you through writing your first eBPF programs using different programming languages and frameworks, providing hands-on experience and practical examples. Chapter 6 explains the crucial aspects of eBPF portability and deployment, introducing **BPF Type Format** (BTF) and **Compile Once, Run Everywhere** (CO-RE) for building and deploying eBPF programs at scale.

The next three chapters take the theoretical knowledge that has been learned so far and demonstrate the practical applications of eBPF. Chapter 7 focuses on eBPF observability, focusing on tracing and analyzing system behavior with minimal overhead. Chapter 8 explores eBPF networking, covering a wide range of program types and their use cases in multiple levels of the Linux network stack including load-balancing, traffic shaping, and socket filtering. Chapter 9 examines the security applications of eBPF, discussing how it can be leveraged for implementing controls and monitoring system activity.

Finally, Chapter 10 provides a look into the future of eBPF, detailing the growing open-source ecosystem, standardization efforts, and emerging trends.

Whether you are a software engineer, a network engineer, a security professional, or simply curious about this emerging technology, This book will be a valuable resource for anyone seeking to understand, explore, and master the eBPF ecosystem.

Chapter 1: Classic Berkeley Packet Filter - This chapter provides a comprehensive introduction to the **classic Berkeley Packet Filter** (**cBPF**), tracing its evolution from its origins in the 1990s as a high-performance network filtering tool. It explores the architecture of cBPF, including its components like the network tap, packet filter, and pseudo-machine, and how they interact to efficiently process network packets. The chapter also delves into the implementation of cBPF in Linux, providing code examples and demonstrating its original uses. It also discusses early applications of cBPF such as tcpdump, and the modernization efforts like JIT compilation and seccomp-bpf that laid the groundwork for the emergence of **extended BPF (eBPF)**.

Chapter 2: Extended Berkeley Packet Filter - This chapter explores the evolution of the **Berkeley Packet Filter (BPF)** to eBPF. It details the history of eBPF, highlighting the challenges and motivations behind its development. The chapter explores the key features of eBPF, emphasizing its efficiency, versatility, and safety advantages over traditional kernel modules. It also provides a comparative analysis of eBPF and cBPF architectures, outlining the advancements in the instruction set, register size, and program loading capabilities. The chapter concludes by examining the differences in virtual machine implementations, the role of the eBPF verifier and JIT compiler, and the functionalities of eBPF helpers and maps.

Chapter 3: eBPF Programming Concepts - This chapter provides an overview of eBPF programming concepts, focusing on the key elements involved in writing eBPF programs. It begins by introducing the bpf() system call, the primary interface for user-space interaction with the eBPF subsystem. It then explains each eBPF program type, exploring the different categories and their specific purposes, along with the corresponding attach types that determine where these programs hook into the kernel. The chapter also examines eBPF maps, detailing their role as efficient key-value stores for inter-process communication, and the various map types available. Additionally, it explores eBPF helper functions and discusses other program primitives such as loops, tail calls, and return codes.

Chapter 4: eBPF Programming Libraries and Frameworks - This chapter explores various libraries and frameworks available for eBPF program development. It discusses the advantages and disadvantages of writing raw BPF bytecode and then introduces libbpf, a core library offering high-level and low-level APIs for interacting with eBPF programs and maps. The chapter also covers the integration of eBPF with the perf profiling tool, enabling advanced tracing capabilities. Furthermore, it examines BCC, a popular framework with a rich collection of tools and examples, and bpftrace, which provides a high-level language for simplified eBPF program creation. Additionally, the chapter explores several Go and Rust libraries like gobpf, ebpf-go, libbpfgo, libbpf-rs, and Aya, offering diverse options for eBPF development in different programming languages. Finally, it touches upon eBPF for Windows, demonstrating the growing cross-platform support for eBPF.

Chapter 5: Writing Your First eBPF Program - This chapter provides a practical guide to writing your first eBPF programs using various programming languages and frameworks. It starts by outlining the necessary steps to set up your development environment, including configuring kernel settings for eBPF functionality. Then, it dives into programming with BCC in Python, demonstrating how to write a simple "Hello World" program using kprobesand a more complex example utilizing maps and helper functions to count syscalls. The chapter also explores writing eBPF programs in C with libbpf, showcasing the process of creating, loading, and attaching BPF programs, along with using maps and helpers. Furthermore, it provides examples of eBPF development in Go using ebpf-go and in Rust using libbpf-rs, highlighting the unique features and functionalities of each framework. Finally, the chapter concludes with a discussion on best practices for writing efficient and safe eBPF programs.

Chapter 6: eBPF Portability and Deploying - This chapter focuses on the practical aspects of deploying eBPF programs in production environments, with a particular emphasis on portability and scalability. It introduces **BPF Type Format (BTF)**, a metadata format crucial for program introspection and portability, and **Compile Once, Run Everywhere (CO-RE)**, a technology that allows eBPF programs to be compiled once and run across different kernel versions without recompilation. The chapter also provides an overview of bpftool, a command-line utility for managing and interacting with eBPF programs and maps. It then delves into different deployment approaches, contrasting the naive method using BCC with the more robust CO-RE-based approach for production systems. Finally, the chapter discusses deployment frameworks like systemd and bpfman, highlighting their features and capabilities for managing eBPF programs at scale, and concludes by emphasizing the importance of feature compatibility, privilege management, unit testing, and staggered deployments for successful production implementation.

Chapter 7: eBPF Observability - This chapter explores the use of eBPF for observability, detailing how its high-performance, low-overhead characteristics enable deep insights into kernel and application behavior. It introduces various eBPF program types designed for observability, including kprobes, uprobes, tracepoints, and perf events, each with its own strengths and use cases. The chapter also examines libbpf tracing macros that simplify eBPF program development and discusses the advantages and disadvantages of using eBPF for tracing compared to other methods. Finally, it provides guidance on selecting the appropriate eBPF program type based on specific needs and performance considerations.

Chapter 8: eBPF Networking - This chapter provides a comprehensive overview of eBPF's applications in networking, showcasing its versatility and capabilities in enhancing network functionality and performance. It explores 18 different eBPF program types, each designed to address specific networking tasks, ranging from socket filtering and traffic control to XDP programming and segment routing offering practical guidance on their usage. It also provides code examples and further references to aid in understanding and implementing these program types effectively.

Chapter 9: eBPF Security - This chapter focuses on the application of eBPF for security purposes, exploring its ability to provide comprehensive system visibility and implement security controls. It introduces various eBPF program types designed for security monitoring and enforcement, such as controlling cgroup device access, managing sysctl parameters, filtering network traffic within cgroups, and implementing **mandatory access control** (**MAC**) policies. The chapter also examines the strengths of eBPF as a security tool and discusses popular open-source eBPF security projects like Falco, Tetragon, Suricata-eBPF, and Pulsar, highlighting their functionalities and contributions to enhancing system security.

Chapter 10: eBPF Open Source Projects and the Future of eBPF - This chapter explores the growing open-source landscape surrounding eBPF, highlighting key projects and future trends. It begins by examining various language-specific projects that facilitate eBPF program development in C, Go, Python, Rust, and WebAssembly. The chapter then delves into notable open-source projects that leverage eBPF for observability, networking, and security, showcasing the versatility and impact of eBPF across different domains. Finally, it discusses the future of eBPF, including standardization efforts, security enhancements, and the expansion of eBPF to new platforms like Windows, emphasizing the continued growth and evolution of the eBPF ecosystem.

Code Bundle and Coloured Images

Please follow the link to download the
Code Bundle and the *Coloured Images* of the book:

https://rebrand.ly/jbp4kb7

The code bundle for the book is also hosted on GitHub at
https://github.com/bpbpublications/Learning-eBPF.

In case there's an update to the code, it will be updated on the existing GitHub repository.

We have code bundles from our rich catalogue of books and videos available at **https://github.com/bpbpublications**. Check them out!

Errata

We take immense pride in our work at BPB Publications and follow best practices to ensure the accuracy of our content to provide with an indulging reading experience to our subscribers. Our readers are our mirrors, and we use their inputs to reflect and improve upon human errors, if any, that may have occurred during the publishing processes involved. To let us maintain the quality and help us reach out to any readers who might be having difficulties due to any unforeseen errors, please write to us at :

errata@bpbonline.com

Your support, suggestions and feedbacks are highly appreciated by the BPB Publications' Family.

Did you know that BPB offers eBook versions of every book published, with PDF and ePub files available? You can upgrade to the eBook version at www.bpbonline.com and as a print book customer, you are entitled to a discount on the eBook copy. Get in touch with us at :

business@bpbonline.com for more details.

At **www.bpbonline.com**, you can also read a collection of free technical articles, sign up for a range of free newsletters, and receive exclusive discounts and offers on BPB books and eBooks.

Piracy

If you come across any illegal copies of our works in any form on the internet, we would be grateful if you would provide us with the location address or website name. Please contact us at **business@bpbonline.com** with a link to the material.

If you are interested in becoming an author

If there is a topic that you have expertise in, and you are interested in either writing or contributing to a book, please visit **www.bpbonline.com**. We have worked with thousands of developers and tech professionals, just like you, to help them share their insights with the global tech community. You can make a general application, apply for a specific hot topic that we are recruiting an author for, or submit your own idea.

Reviews

Please leave a review. Once you have read and used this book, why not leave a review on the site that you purchased it from? Potential readers can then see and use your unbiased opinion to make purchase decisions. We at BPB can understand what you think about our products, and our authors can see your feedback on their book. Thank you!

For more information about BPB, please visit **www.bpbonline.com**.

Join our book's Discord space

Join the book's Discord Workspace for Latest updates, Offers, Tech happenings around the world, New Release and Sessions with the Authors:

https://discord.bpbonline.com

Table of Contents

CHAPTER 1

Classic Berkeley Packet Filter

Introduction

Berkeley Packet Filter (BPF) (originally known as **Berkeley Software Distribution** (**BSD**) Packet Filter) is a framework originally built around high-performance network filtering and packet capture. It utilizes a **central processing unit** (**CPU**) register-based filter evaluator that runs as a pseudo-machine inside a Unix-based kernel.

Today, the **extended Berkeley Packet Filter** (**eBPF**) is much more than that. It provides low-level observability and high-performance network capabilities on Linux, macOS, and Windows systems, becoming an essential tool for network administrators, security researchers, and software developers. Before we jump into eBPF, it is important to understand the underlying mechanisms behind eBPF, and its evolution over time.

This chapter will introduce BPF, examine the events that led up to its creation in 1992, and explain the architecture of how it works. In this section, we will exclusively evaluate the original implementation of BPF, now known as the **classic Berkeley Packet Filter** (**cBPF**).

Structure

In this chapter, we will go through the following topics:

- Introduction to BPF
- Before BPF, a history
- BPF architecture
- BPF on Linux
- Early BPF usage
- Modernizing BPF before eBPF

Objectives

In this chapter, you will learn the beginnings of cBPF and why it was created, as the architecture of the original BPF **virtual machine** (**VM**). Then you will learn how to write basic cBPF packet filter programs on Linux as well as write basic Seccomp-BPF programs. Finally, you will learn about the efforts to modernize cBPF before the eventual creation of eBPF.

Introduction to BPF

If you think you are new to cBPF, you may not realize that you have likely used cBPF before in the form of **tcpdump** filters. The BPF specification provides a raw interface (as opposed to copying packets across kernel/ user-space boundaries) to data link layers (Layer 2 of the OSI model) in a protocol-independent fashion. All packets on the (L2) network, even those destined for other hosts, are accessible through this mechanism. cBPF allows running user space code (filters) against raw network interfaces inside a sanity-checking virtual machine.

BPF was first implemented in BSD as the BSD Packet Filter, it was later implemented in Linux which was known as Linux Packet Filter or Berkeley Packet Filter. Once BPF was optimized and extended in 2014, the original implementation became known as classic BPF, or cBPF for short.

Before BPF, a history

As *Steven McCanne* and *Van Jacobson*, the creators of BPF note in their 1992 paper *A New Architecture for User-level Packet Capture* (**https://www.tcpdump.org/papers/bpf-usenix93.pdf**), until the creation of

BPF, each flavor of Unix (NIT, SunOS, Uiltrix, SGI were popular at the time) provided different facilities for kernel packet filtering. Even with the significantly slower network speeds in the early 1990s, these implementations were still considered sub-optimal and warranted improvements.

McCanne and *Van Jacobson's* USENIX paper in 1992 described BSD Packet Filter which was a new kernel architecture for packet capture. BPF offered significant performance improvements over the existing packet capture facilities (see *Figure 8* of the paper).

The original BPF implementation (known as BSD Packet Filter) was implemented in BSD Unix, starting in version 4.3 and SunOS in version 3.5. It was not until 1999, in Linux Kernel version 2.1.75, that the Linux Socket Filter, aka BPF, was released.

BPF architecture

This section covers the implementation of BPF as described in *McCanne* and *Van Jacobson's* USENIX paper. As we will go on to discuss, various platforms have implemented BPF with some variety.

BPF works by a user defining a filter (that is program) which is converted to BPF bytecode and then passed to the BPF virtual machine in kernel space for execution by an interpreter as seen in *Figure 1.1.* This allows the filter to be run in kernel-space safely which removes the need for copying all packets across from kernel-space to user-space.

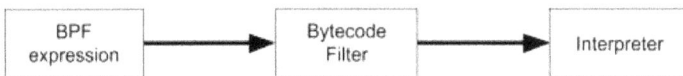

Figure 1.1: *The BPF filter lifecycle*

BPF has three main components (displayed in *Figure 1.2*):

- **Network tap**: Collects copies of packets from the network device drivers and delivers them to listening applications

- **Packet filter**: Decides if a packet should be accepted and how to copy it to the application

- **The BPF pseudo-machine**: The in-kernel VM that runs the BPF filter (i.e. program)

Figure 1.2 illustrates the original BPF architecture and the division between user-space, kernel-space, and the network:

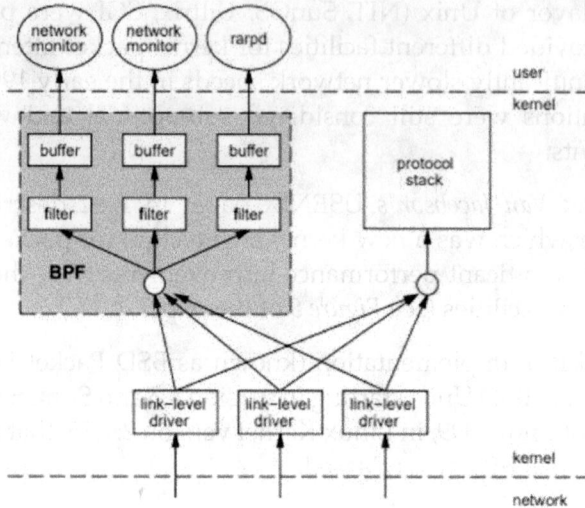

Figure 1.2: The BPF architecture (source: BSD Packet Filter)

Network tap

While a BPF filter (program) is running and the packet arrives at the network interface, instead of being processed via the unix protocol stack (e.g. TCP or UDP), it is first processed by the BPF pseudo-machine. BPF feeds the packet to the user-defined filter(s), aka the BPF filter, where if the filter accepts the packet, it is copied over to the buffer associated with that filter. This is an optimization over all packets having to be copied from kernel-space to user-space and then filtered.

The program listening in user-space reads the packets in the buffer and processes/displays them in the manner that the user-space application defines. The packet then proceeds to be processed by the network stack as normal.

Filter

Until the creation of BPF, there were several filter models in existence: **CMU/ Stanford Packet Filter (CSPF)**, NIT in SunOS, Ultrix Packet Filter in DEC Ultrix and snoop in SGI IRIX. CSPF was one of the more prevalent filter models.

BPF utilizes a **control flow graph (CFG)** filter displayed in *Figure 1.3*, which removes redundant evaluations that are present in the CSPF filter. Each node in the graph is a comparison predicate with two final targets (true/false). This is easier to model on registers. There is a one-time overhead to order/optimize the graph.

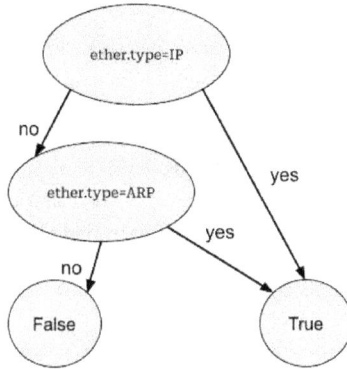

Figure 1.3: *Simple CFG of a ip or arp filter (source: BSD Packet Filter)*

While the above example is simple, you can see in this more complex filter example, shown in *Figure 1.4*.

You can see in this example, there is a maximum of 5 evaluation operations.

If this same filter were to be written using CSPF, there would be a minimum (and maximum) of 7 evaluation operations (as shown in *Figure 1.4*):

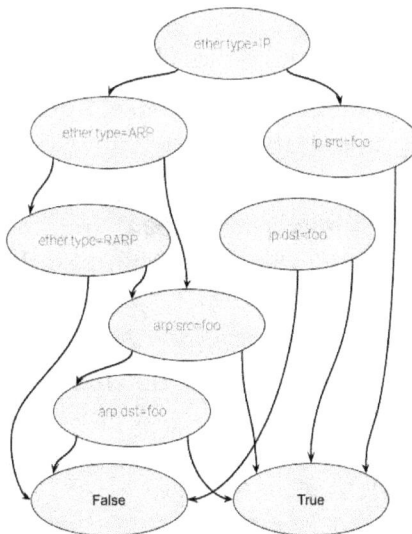

Figure 1.4: *CFG of a host foo filter (source: BSD Packet Filter)*

The CFG filter model is superior in its efficiency, especially as the complexity of the filter expression increases. You can read more about the performance improvements the CFG and BPF model provides in the *McCane* paper.

libpcap

libpcap is a well-known library that converts BPF syntax (e.g. dst host 198.51.100.200) to BPF bytecode filters. If you want to see this for yourself, you can use the **-dd** option in **tcpdump** to print the filter in an assembly code program fragment as shown in *Example 1.1*.

Example 1.1: **tcpdump** BPF bytecode filter:

```
$ sudo tcpdump -i en0 -dd 'ip and tcp'
(000) ldh      [12]
(001) jeq  #0x0800 jt 2 jf 5
(002) ldb      [23]
(003) jeq  #0x6    jt 4 jf 5
(004) ret        #262144
(005) ret        #0
```

The program runs as follows:

1. Load a half-word (2 bytes) from the current packet at offset **12** (the EtherType ethernet frame field).

2. Check if the EtherType value is 0x0800 which is an IPv4 packet and if so go to instruction 2, otherwise (fail and) jump to instruction 5 (**005**) and return 0.

3. Load a byte from the packet at offset **23** of the ethernet packet. This is the protocol field 9 bytes within an IP header.

4. Check if the value of the field is 0x06 which is the TCP protocol. If true, jump to instruction 4 (**004**), trim the packet to 262144 bytes, and return it. Otherwise, jump to instruction 5 (**005**) and return 0.

The BPF exam tool allows you to examine the process of building and optimizing BPF packet filters. In the section *BPF on Linux*, we will write our first BPF program that performs basic packet filtering.

BPF pseudo-machine

The BPF pseudo-machine is a (32 bit) register-based virtual machine (even on 64-bit machines), consisting of an accumulator, an index register (known as X), a scratch memory store (16 slots), and an implicit program counter (known as A). It has a small set of arithmetic, logical, and jump instructions. The accumulator is used for arithmetic operations, while the index register provides offsets into the packet or the scratch memory areas.

The operations of the machine can be categorized into the following groups:

- Load instructions
- Store instructions
- Arithmetic or logic instructions
- Branch instructions
- Return instructions
- Miscellaneous instructions

Instruction set and addressing modes

The cBPF VM has a limited instruction set (22 to be exact) as shown in *Table 1.1*:

opcodes	Addr modes				
ldb	[k]			[x + k]	
ldh	[k]			[x + k]	
ld	#k	# len	M [k]	[k]	[x + k]
ldx	#k	# len	M [k]	[k]	[x + k]
st	M [k]				
stx	M [k]				
jmp	L				
jeq	#k, Lt, Lf				
jgt	#k, Lt, Lf				
jge	#k, Lt, Lf				
jset	#k, Lt, Lf				
add	# k		x		
sub	# k		x		
mul	# k		x		
div	# k		x		

opcodes	Addr modes		
and	# k		x
or	# k		x
lsh	# k		x
rsh	# k		x
ret	# k		a
tax			
txa			

Table 1.1: The BPF instruction set (source: BSD Packet Filter)

The definition of the opcodes is as follows:

- **ldb, ldh, ld**: Load into the accumulator
- **ldx**: Load into the index register
- **add, sub, mul, dev**: Perform arithmetic with the accumulator and operand and store the return into the accumulator
- **jset**: Performs a bitwise AND
- **jmp**: Jump instructions (both for true and false cases)
- **jeq, jgt, jge**: Equality check, greater than check, greater than equal check
- **ret**: Return
- **tax/txa**: Copy A into X/ Copy X into A

The addressing modes for the BPF machine are described as follows in *Table 1.2:*

# k	The literal value stored in k
# len	The length of the packet
M [k]	The word at the offset k in the scratch memory store
[k]	The bye, halfword, or word at byte offset k in the packet
[x + k]	The bute, halfword, or word at offset $x + k$ in the packet
L	The offset from the current instruction to L
#k, Lt, Lf	The offset to Lt if the predicate is true, otherwise the offset to Lf

x	The index register
4 * ([k]&0xf)	Four times the value of the low four bites of the byte at offset *k* in the packet

Table 1.2: *BPF addressing mode (source: BSD Packet Filter)*

As noted earlier, the ability to jump to different instructions based on true/false conditions.

The instruction format is displayed in *Table 1.3,* with the number of bits in the instruction being the integer (note the use of 32 bits for the k register):

opcode: 16	jt: 8	jf: 8
k: 32		

Table 1.3: *BPF instruction format (source: BSD Packet Filter)*

- The opcode field represents the instruction type and the addressing mode.

- The jt and jf fields are used by the conditional jump instructions and represent the offsets from the next instruction to the true and false target

- The k field is used for various purposes per the addressing modes

Features of BPF

With this new in-kernel VM, cBPF brought several new features to end users that they did not have available previously:

- **High-performance packet capture**: cBPF provides a mechanism for capturing packets at high speed, allowing administrators to capture large volumes of network traffic without impacting the performance of the system. At the time that the cBPF paper was written, this was a very large advantage of this system.

- **Flexible filtering rules**: cBPF provides a flexible way to define filtering rules that can be based on a wide range of criteria, including source and destination addresses, protocol types, port numbers, and more.

- **Real-time filtering**: cBPF allows administrators to filter packets in real-time, enabling them to detect security threats and troubleshoot network performance issues as they occur.

- **Low overhead**: cBPF has a low overhead, which means that it can capture and filter packets with minimal impact on system performance.

BPF on Linux

BPF was implemented in Linux in 1999 and released in Linux kernel version 2.1.75 as **Linux Socket Filter (LSF)**.

LSF is derived from the BPF and while the implementation is somewhat different, many of the mechanisms remain the same. With LSF, you can simply attach your BPF program filter to a socket via the **SO_ATTACH_FILTER** socket option. Sockets are utilized for passing/ receiving packets to/ from kernel-space instead of using buffers.

Installing prerequisites packages

Before we get started with writing programs, we are going to install all the prerequisites for writing cBPF and eBPF programs. You can do this by running the following command on a Linux machine:

```
$ sudo apt install -y make gcc libpcap-dev
```

How LSF applications work

1. A special purpose socket is created of **PF_PACKET** domain, **SOCK_RAW** type.

2. A BPF program is attached to the socket using the **setsockopt**(2) system call and the **SO_ATTACH_FILTER** socket option.

3. (Optionally) The socket is set to promiscuous mode using ioctl(2).

4. Reading/sending packets to/from the kernel (via the socket) is done via the **recv**(2)/ **send**(2) system calls.

You can see an example of the previous four steps below (adapted from the LSF documentation). In this example, we are going to attach a filter to all interfaces that prints the bytes of packets that match the **tcpdump** filter of **ip and tcp** (*Example 1.2*).

Example 1.2: Example BPF program that prints TCP/IP packets (**ch01/ lsf.c**):

```
int main(int argc, char *argv[]) {
    int sockfd, ret, iface_idx;
    struct sock_fprog filter;
    struct sock_filter code[] = {
        { 0x28, 0, 0, 0x0000000c },
        { 0x15, 0, 3, 0x00000800 },
        { 0x30, 0, 0, 0x00000017 },
        { 0x15, 0, 1, 0x00000006 },
        { 0x6, 0, 0, 0x00040000 },
        { 0x6, 0, 0, 0x00000000 },
    };
    /* Open raw socket */
    sockfd = socket(PF_PACKET, SOCK_RAW, htons(ETH_P_ALL));
    if (sockfd == -1) {
        perror("socket");
        exit(EXIT_FAILURE);
    }

    /* Set filter program */
    filter.len = sizeof(code)/sizeof(code[0]);
    filter.filter = code;
    ret = setsockopt(sockfd, SOL_SOCKET, SO_ATTACH_FILTER,
&filter, sizeof(filter));
    if (ret == -1) {
        perror("setsockopt");
        exit(EXIT_FAILURE);
    }
```

In the first part of this example, we create a BPF filter program to only return packets that match **ip and tcp**. We then create a **SOCK_RAW** socket and then attach the BPF filter to that socket using **setsockopt**:

```
    /* Receive and print TCP packets */
    char buffer[4096];
    ssize_t len;
    struct ethhdr *eth_hdr;
    struct iphdr *ip_hdr;
    struct tcphdr *tcp_hdr;
    while (1) {
```

```
        len = recv(sockfd, buffer, sizeof(buffer), 0);
        if (len == -1) {
            perror("recv");
            exit(EXIT_FAILURE);
        }
        eth_hdr = (struct ethhdr *)buffer;

        /* Parse IP header */
        ip_hdr = (struct iphdr *)(buffer + sizeof(struct
ethhdr));

        /* Parse TCP header */
        tcp_hdr = (struct tcphdr *)(buffer + sizeof(struct
ethhdr) + sizeof(struct iphdr));

        if (ntohs(eth_hdr->h_proto) == ETH_P_IP && ip_hdr-
>protocol == IPPROTO_TCP) {
            printf("Received TCP packet from %s:%d to
%s:%d\n",

                inet_ntoa(*(struct in_addr *)&ip_hdr-
>saddr),

                ntohs(tcp_hdr->source),
                inet_ntoa(*(struct in_addr *)&ip_hdr-
>daddr),

                ntohs(tcp_hdr->dest));

        }
    }
    /* Close the socket */
    close(sockfd);
}
```

On the user-space side, we create a loop that continually reads the filtered data from the socket and then parses the data and printers which the TCP packet was received from.

We can run and compile the program in the following manner:

```
$ gcc lsf.c -o lsf -lpcap
$ chmod +x lsf
$ sudo ./lsf
```

```
Received TCP packet from 192.168.1.237:3001 to
192.168.1.237:48302
Received TCP packet from 192.168.1.100:48302 to
192.168.1.100:3001
Received TCP packet from 192.168.1.237:3001 to
192.168.1.237:48302
Received TCP packet from 192.168.1.100:48302 to
192.168.1.100:3001
```

Once you compile and run the program, it prints a new line for each set of packets we receive. In this case, we do some basic parsing of the packet to extract the source and destination IP and ports and print them. Congratulations, you have now written your first BPF program!

Of course, writing the BPF filter bytecode can be tedious if not downright impractical. So, we can utilize **libpcap** to write the BPF filter for us.

Example 1.3: Example BPF program that prints TCP/ IP packets (**ch01/lsf2.c**):

```c
int main(int argc, char *argv[]) {

    int sockfd, ret;
    char* filter_string = argv[1];
    char errbuf[PCAP_ERRBUF_SIZE];
    struct sock_fprog filter;
    struct bpf_program fp;
    pcap_t* handle;

    // Compile the filter expression
    handle = pcap_open_dead(DLT_RAW, 65535);
    if (handle == NULL) {
        fprintf(stderr, "Couldn't open device: %s\n",
errbuf);
        exit(EXIT_FAILURE);
    }
    if (pcap_compile(handle, &fp, filter_string, 0, PCAP_
NETMASK_UNKNOWN) == -1) {
        fprintf(stderr, "Couldn't parse filter %s: %s\n",
filter_string, pcap_geterr(handle));
        exit(EXIT_FAILURE);
```

```
    }
    pcap_close(handle);

    // Convert the BPF program to sock_fprog
    filter.len = fp.bf_len;
    filter.filter = (struct sock_filter *) fp.bf_insns;

    sockfd = socket(PF_PACKET, SOCK_RAW, htons(ETH_P_ALL));
    if (sockfd == -1) {
        perror("socket");
        exit(EXIT_FAILURE);
    }

    /* Set filter program */
    filter.len = sizeof(code)/sizeof(code[0]);
    filter.filter = code;
    ret = setsockopt(sockfd, SOL_SOCKET, SO_ATTACH_FILTER,
&filter, sizeof(filter));
```

In this example, we create a **pcap** handler that we would not actually use to capture packets using **pcap_open_dead()** and then **pcap_compile()** to take the filter expression (for example, tcp and ip) and turn it into a BPF filter.

We will talk more about writing and building your own programs in *Chapter 5, Writing Your First eBPF Program*.

Early BPF usage

As noted earlier, the most well-known application of BPF is tcpdump. tcpdump allows you to write expressive filters and have them compiled by **libpcap** library when invoking the program.

Other applications that have used BPF, per the 1992 *McCane* paper:

- arpwatch
- netload & histo
- reverse ARP daemon
- nnstat
- nswatch

Modernizing BPF before eBPF

Between the initial introduction of BPF to Linux and the eventual move to eBPF in Linux 3.15, there were some updates made to BPF in Linux that made it more robust and useful.

JIT

In Linux version 3.0, *Eric Dumazet* made a patch that added a **just-in-time** (**JIT**) compiler to the kernel to allow the kernel to translate BPF code directly into the host system's assembly code. The simplicity of the BPF machine makes the JIT translation relatively simple; every BPF instruction maps to a straightforward x86 instruction sequence.

Seccomp-BPF

SECure COMPuting (**Seccomp**) provides a method to specify a filter which system calls (and arguments) are available to a userland process to execute. It was first introduced into Linux in 2.6.12. As this *LWN.net* article (**https://lwn.net/Articles/475043/**) notes, this was not particularly successful.

In Linux 3.5, seccomp-BPF was introduced. Instead of a fixed and very limited set of system calls, seccomp has evolved into a filtering mechanism that allows processes to specify an arbitrary filter of system calls (expressed as a cBPF program) that should be forbidden. Seccomp is utilized in modern browsers to create a sandbox around the browser and not allow access to the system.

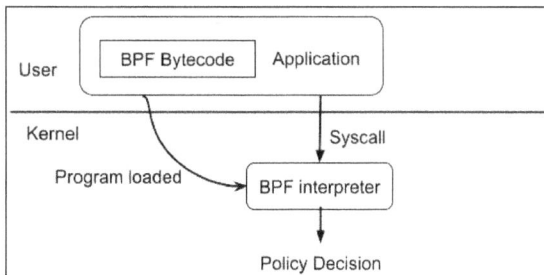

Figure 1.5: Seccomp-bpf architecture

This functionality quickly made it into systemd which allows you to specify a list of syscalls available to the unit via the property `SystemCallFilter`. For example:

```
[Service]
ExecStart=/bin/echo "I am in a sandbox"
SystemCallFilter=brk mmap access open fstat close read fstat
mprotect arch_prctl munmap write
```

Today, you can also write your own programs and utilize seccomp-bpf to provide protection as to what syscalls are available. In this example, we define a BPF seccomp program that allows only the **stat** syscall and does not allow the **open** syscall.

Example 1.4: Example seccomp-bpf example that does not allow you to run the **open** syscall:

```
int main() {
    int ret;
    char *file_path = "/etc/passwd";
    struct stat stats;
    struct sock_filter filter[] = {
        /* Load architecture */
        BPF_STMT(BPF_LD | BPF_W | BPF_ABS, 4),
        BPF_JUMP(BPF_JMP | BPF_JEQ | BPF_K, ARCH_NR, 0, 1),
        /* Load system call number */
        BPF_STMT(BPF_LD | BPF_W | BPF_ABS, 0),
        /* Deny open syscall */
        BPF_JUMP(BPF_JMP | BPF_JEQ | BPF_K, __NR_openat, 0,
1),
        BPF_STMT(BPF_RET | BPF_K, SECCOMP_RET_TRAP),
        /* Allow everything else */
        BPF_STMT(BPF_RET | BPF_K, SECCOMP_RET_ALLOW),
    };
    struct sock_fprog prog = {
        .len = sizeof(filter)/sizeof(filter[0]),
        .filter = filter,
    };

    /* Load the filter */
    if (prctl(PR_SET_NO_NEW_PRIVS, 1, 0, 0, 0)) {
        perror("prctl(NO_NEW_PRIVS)");
        return 1;
```

```c
    }
    ret = prctl(PR_SET_SECCOMP, SECCOMP_MODE_FILTER, &prog);
    if (ret < 0) {
        perror("prctl");
        exit(EXIT_FAILURE);
    }

    /* Try to stat the file */
    ret = stat(file_path, &stats);
    if (ret < 0) {
        perror("stat");
        exit(EXIT_FAILURE);
    } else {
        printf("stat succeeded\n");
    }

    /* Try to open the file */
    int fd = open(file_path, O_RDONLY);
    // Program should error-out here
    if (fd > 0) {
        printf("open succeeded, should not have
happened\n");
        close(fd);
    }
    return 0;
}
```

You can compile and run the program using the following commands:

```
$ gcc seccomp_example.c -o seccomp_example
$ ./seccomp_example
stat succeeded
Bad system call
```

In this example, the BPF program is loaded and allows the program to **stat /etc/password**, but not to open (specifically the **'openat'** **syscall**) **/etc/passwd**.

A seccomp-BPF program must return one of the following error codes as defined in **usr/include/linux/seccomp.h.**

Example 1.5: Seccomp-BPF error codes:

```
#define SECCOMP_RET_KILL_PROCESS 0x80000000U /* kill the
process */
#define SECCOMP_RET_KILL_THREAD  0x00000000U /* kill the
thread */
#define SECCOMP_RET_KILL        SECCOMP_RET_KILL_THREAD
#define SECCOMP_RET_TRAP        0x00030000U /* disallow and
force a SIGSYS */
#define SECCOMP_RET_ERRNO       0x00050000U /* returns an
errno */
#define SECCOMP_RET_USER_NOTIF  0x7fc00000U /* notifies
userspace */
#define SECCOMP_RET_TRACE       0x7ff00000U /* pass to a
tracer or disallow */
#define SECCOMP_RET_LOG         0x7ffc0000U /* allow after
logging */
#define SECCOMP_RET_ALLOW       0x7fff0000U /* allow */
```

In this example, we have returned **SECCOMP_RET_ALLOW** to allow any syscall that is not **openat**. When the **openat syscall** is called, the program returns **SECCOMP_RET_TRAP**. We can also modify the BPF to return a specific error code if the syscall is not allowed:

```
BPF_STMT(BPF_RET | BPF_K, SECCOMP_RET_ERRNO | (EPERM &
SECCOMP_RET_DATA))
```

If the filter is going to deny the syscall, then the program can return the **EPERM** error code and the user application can catch the example specifically.

As we will discuss further in *Chapter 8, eBPF Networking*, BPF can be used extensively to detect and protect against malicious activity.

BPF+

In 1999, *Andrew Begel, Steven McCanne* (the original BPF author), and *Susan L. Graham* proposed BPF+, an optimized implementation of BPF filters. BPF+ focused on optimizing the filter program and adding a JIT filter. None of the optimizations ever made it into programs/libraries like **libpcap**, however, they became key features of eBPF many years later:

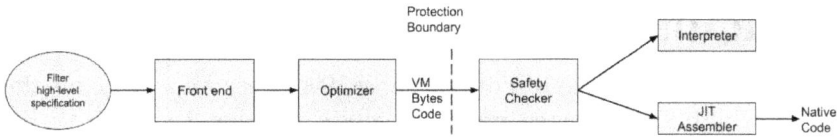

Figure 1.6: *The BPF+ architecture*

While retaining much of the same structure as the original BPF design, BPF+ foreshadowed several key improvements that would be implemented nearly 15 years later.

The key aspects that changed were:

- The paper proposed an upgraded filter language specification, arguing that the current tcpdump like filter syntax was too primitive and burdensome for the end-user to write complex queries. For example, the authors proposed queries like TCP port HTTP (i.e., tcp and port 80) or src network MIT and dst network UCD.

- The BPF compiler or frontend as described in this paper, would be split from the optimizer allowing for different programming frameworks to compile the application before having a common optimizer framework.

- The compiler will output the program in **Static Single Assignment** (**SSA**) form which is then fed to an optimizer which outputs the in bytecode format, which is **Reduce Instruction Set Computer** (**RISC**)-like register-based variant of the original BPF VM.

- Once the bytecode is injected into kernel-space, there is another safety verifier which ensures the program does not have any infinite loops or would cause memory errors via illegal instructions.

- Then a JIT assembler translates the optimized/verified bytecode into native machine code and may perform machine-dependent optimization.

As you will read in *Chapter 2, Extended Berkeley Packet Filter*, many of these concepts were adopted into the eBPF ecosystem.

Conclusion

The introduction of the BPF in the early 1990s became a fundamental part of high-performance packet analysis and led the way to the introduction of running custom code inside the kernel. The model of inserting custom code into the kernel and running it safely was a game changer for network engineers trying to capture packets and debug network issues. Remarkably, this functionality remained largely untouched in Linux for nearly 15 years until the introduction of eBPF in 2013.

In the next chapter, we are going to introduce eBPF and explain the evolution of cBPF to eBPF.

Join our book's Discord space

Join the book's Discord Workspace for Latest updates, Offers, Tech happenings around the world, New Release and Sessions with the Authors:

https://discord.bpbonline.com

CHAPTER 2
Extended Berkeley Packet Filter

Introduction

Extended Berkeley Packet Filter (**eBPF**) is the evolution of cBPF, providing a powerful platform to write high-throughput, low overhead; tracing, filtering, security, and network programs. eBPF's highly efficient design has made it a popular technology to build real-time monitoring and tracing systems. Furthermore, the low-level hooks into the kernel also provide mechanisms to perform security enforcement and highly performant network functions.

In this chapter, we will introduce the eBPF, discuss how it came to fruition, its features, the platform's architecture, and how it differs from cBPF.

Structure

In this chapter, we will learn the following topics:

- Introduction to eBPF
- History of eBPF
- Need of eBPF

- Features of eBPF
- eBPF use cases
- eBPF concepts
- eBPF architecture
- Differences between BPF and eBPF

Objectives

In this chapter, you will learn about how eBPF was created and why it was needed. You will learn its specific feature set and use cases and then learn the architecture and implementation differences between cBPF and eBPF.

Introducing eBPF

In 2013, *Alexei Starovoitov* proposed a major rewrite of BPF, and *Daniel Borkmann* introduced the eBPF into the Linux kernel in 2014 (version 3.15).

Starovoitov's contributions to the Linux kernel optimized the BPF instruction set and hence paved the way to not only improve network filter performance but eventually change the landscape of Linux observability, **software-defined networks** (**SDN**), and enhanced security monitoring programs. Since the initial commit in 2013, the eBPF system has been constantly updated to add new features and has become one of the most popular spaces in kernel and systems development over the past decade.

eBPF extends the capabilities of BPF by allowing developers to write and inject custom programs into kernel space, which can be used for a wide range of tasks beyond packet filtering. Its programs can be attached to various kernel events, such as system calls, network traffic, and file operations, and can be used to perform a wide range of tasks, such as profiling, debugging, and security enforcement.

History of eBPF

At the *2022 Kernel Recipes* conference, *Starovoitov* spoke about the origins of eBPF and how his team at Plumgrid decided on the eBPF design.

At that time, writing kernel modules (custom modules that are compiled and enabled) was the popular way to take your custom code and have it run in the kernel. The team proposed writing their kernel module to perform SDN functions on a virtual machine. Their initial solution was to create one kernel module that performed switching, routing, firewalling, as well as NAT, load balancing, and packet capture. While this was initially fruitful, the team quickly ran into stability issues due to memory limitations in the x86 architecture implementation.

The second iteration was to write a verifier function to ensure strict memory safety before loading the kernel module into the kernel. While this was helpful, it was still overly complex due to the large instruction set that x86 runs. There are a lot of ways to compute memory addresses and to access memory. Creating a verifier that could cover all of these cases is exceptionally challenging.

The solution involved restricting the instructions that the kernel module could use, which was achieved by modifying the **GNU Compiler Collection** (**GCC**) backend to impose limitations on the program instructions. The first kernel module that Plumgrid released had a verifier but lacked JIT safety measures.

The next attempt was to create the instruction set that the program would use and get GCC to output bytecode directly upon compilation. The team bundled the verifier with a new JIT safety checker. The team had a working solution! However, they had to upstream their work into the Linux kernel but met strong resistance from kernel maintainers, which eventually led to them abandoning this approach.

The team realized that their new instruction set approach was not as novel as they had initially thought, as it bore notable resemblances to other instruction sets already present in the kernel, specifically BPF, iptables, and netfilter tables. They recognized the importance of aligning their work closely with cBPF and decided to reuse the opcode encoding, build an 8-byte instruction, and call it eBPF.

After getting acquainted with the kernel netdev kernel mailing list, *Alexei* started to build a reputation amongst kernel maintainers by submitting patches to fix deadlocks, race conditions, etc. With this newfound reputation, he posted the eBPF patchset. Unfortunately, the patchset was rejected at the time due to concerns with changes to the kernel **User Application Programming Interface** (**UAPI**). He tried to add eBPF to the kernel without changing the UAPI. *Alexei* first looked at the cBPF interpreter, rewrote it with his eBPF instruction set, and made cBPF 2 times faster. This implementation was named internal BPF.

By May of 2014, BPF had a cBPF to eBPF converter. The interpreter was running iBPF and x86, sparc, arm had JIT compilers that converted iBPF to native code. However, there was no verifier at this time.

The Plumgrid team wanted to add the verifier as well as helpers, maps, and hook programs to the **netif_recieve_skb** kernel function. At that time, he faced significant resistance and pushback due to concerns that eBPF might circumvent the kernel networking stack.

Not to be discouraged, they pivoted to create a filter for perf events, which gave them a way to incorporate the verifier, as well as maps and helpers concepts, and have the BPF programs triggered by kprobes and perf events.

With a small win under their belt, the team tried to replace the TC u32 classifier with a BPF classifier, as the BPF one was faster. Some compromises had to be made with the design to get it up-streamed into the kernel. On September 26th, 2014, 6 patches were accepted into the kernel that added a verifier, BPF maps, as well as the **bpf()** syscall. The initial concept of eBPF in the Linux kernel had been realized.

A few months later, the new BPF program types were made available:

- Socket filters (December 1st 2014)
- TC classifier (March 1st 2015)
- Tracing (kprobe) and perf (March 25th, 2015)

Once these patches were in, projects like **https://github.com/iovisor/BCC** were started and so began the era of high-performance programmable tracing.

Need of eBPF

Until eBPF was implemented, the functionality of BPF was limited to network packet filtering and later on, Seccomp-BPF. With the advancement of systems in the 1990s and 2000s, gaining speed and increased software complexity, there emerged a growing necessity to effectively observe, debug, and comprehend these systems. eBPF fills that need by providing high-performance, low-overhead functionality without the need to use kernel modules or worry about kernel panics because of unsafe code.

In the later chapters of this book, we will explore how traditional load-balancing, firewalling, and security paradigms faced escalating management challenges in the early 2010s, ultimately becoming highly unscalable. eBPF has effectively addressed this need for numerous companies.

Today, eBPF has become a new utility in not only packet filtering, but also providing extensive Linux observability capabilities, and network and security abilities that power some of the world's most used software products.

Features of eBPF

eBPF has gained notoriety as a platform because it has a number of key features over the existing technologies like kernel modules. Some of these include:

- eBPF programs are highly efficient and are optimized before being run inside kernel space. This makes it ideal for real-time monitoring and analysis of kernel tasks, particularly network traffic.

- eBPF can be used for a multitude of applications including security monitoring and enforcement, low-level kernel debugging as well as load-balancing and network intrusion detection.

- eBPF's JIT verifier performs safety checks of the code that gets injected into the kernel and prevents illegal instructions from being executed. This safety is an important upgrade from the behavior of kernel modules which can cause difficult to debug kernel panics while executing illegal instructions.

- eBPF code is portable and can be compiled across distributions and architectures. We will discuss it in *Chapter 6, eBPF Portability and Deploying*.

- eBPF can be written using a number of programming languages and is relatively easy to learn. Projects like **iovisor/bcc** make it super easy to get started.

eBPF use cases

As we have briefly discussed earlier in this chapter, eBPF is exceptionally flexible and can be used in a range of various applications. Some applications include:

- **Packet filtering**: Carrying on from the foundations in cBPF, eBPF's first program type was a packet filter.

- **System tracing and analysis**: EBPF provides a number of avenues to perform low-overhead tracing in both kernel and user space.

- **Network intrusion detection systems (IDS), intrusion prevention systems (IPS)**: The introduction of the **eXpress Data Path** (**XDP**) program type has revolutionized high-performance software defined networking. Many hyperscalers now depend on eBPF XDP programs to perform critical load-balancing and security functions on their edge networks.

- **Security**: EBPF can also be utilized in a number of ways to improve system security in both bare-metal and containerized environments.

We will review all of these use cases in depth in *Chapters 7, eBPF Observability, Chapter 8, eBPF Networking,* and *Chapter 9, eBPF Security.*

eBPF concepts

Before we review the improved eBPF architecture, let us look at some of the new key concepts of eBPF:

- **BPF instructions**: These are bytecode program instructions to be executed by the BPF VM, similar to the BPF bytecode we examined in *Chapter 1, Classic Berkeley Packet Filter*. Currently, the maximum number of instructions is 4096 per program, but it can be altered by configuring your own kernel.

- **BPF verifier**: Optimizes the program and verifies it is safe for execution:

  o Checks **directed acyclic graph** (**DAG**) for unbounded loops.

  o Ensure there are no loops or invalid/bad pointer de-references.

- o   Move cold blocks out of the critical path.

- o   Utilizing `likely()`/`unlikely()` hints provides extra performance.

- **BPF hooks (attach types)**: BPF programs attach to specific events in the kernel that trigger the execution of the BPF program. We will discuss it in *Chapter 3, eBPF Programming Concepts.*

- **BPF JIT**: After the verifier verifies the BPF instructions, the JIT compiler verifies the program again and compiles that into instructions native to the CPU architecture.

- **BPF helpers**: These are in-kernel helper functions that enable BPF functionality (`map_lookup` /`update` /`delete` as well as other general-purpose functions that are only available from within eBPF programs.)

- **BPF maps**: Key/value storage of different data types — userspace can read/write these maps

- **BPF syscall**: This is the bpf syscall that is used for interactions between user space and kernel space.

You can see many of these concepts in the following figure, showing the representation of the eBPF architecture:

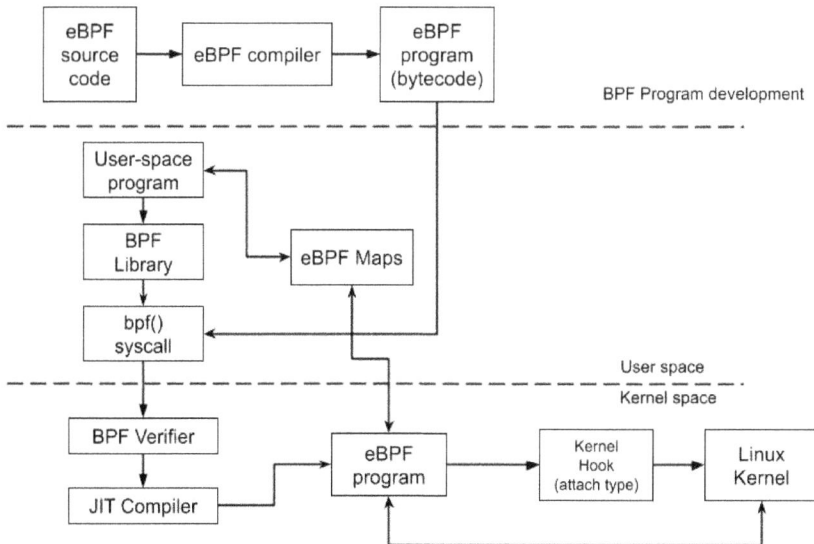

Figure 2.1: The eBPF architecture

eBPF architecture

eBPF builds off BPF, adding a 64-bit **Reduced Instruction Set Computer (RISC)** instruction set with a larger number of registers and by default includes a JIT compiler that has access to a subset of kernel functions (see more about this in *Chapter 3, eBPF Programming Concepts*).

One of the largest benefits of eBPF is that you can run arbitrary code in kernel space, not just packet filters. There is a caveat to this as you need to attach your program to a particular event in the kernel (kprobes, sockets, perf events) known as an **attach-type**. Alternatively, you can also attach eBPF programs to network sockets and cgroups to perform packet classification, filtering, and forwarding.

An eBPF program can hook into various kernel events (kprobes, syscalls, **User Defined Static Tracepoints (UDST's)**). The program can also read and write data into an in-memory structure called a map. This map is available to be read by the corresponding program running in user space.

Conversely, it can be used to process network packets and perform load-balancing, **distributed denial of service (DDOS)** protection, and firewalling functions with exceptionally high performance.

The lifecycle of an eBPF program is similar to cBPF program:

1. An eBPF program is written and then compiled into BPF bytecode using a GCC, **Low Level Virtual Machine (LLVM)**, or Clang compiler.

2. The program is then loaded into the eBPF VM using the bpf(2) syscall.

3. The eBPF VM verifies the code and runs a JIT compiler before converting it to native instruction code and running the program.

eBPF offers the benefit of being both fast and secure.

The architecture of cBPF and eBPF, while similar, has significantly evolved. There is now a runtime JIT compiler and verifier to ensure the safety of the program (things BPF+ advocated for).

The steps for running an eBPF program are:

1. User-space sends bytecode to the kernel together with a program type which determines what kernel areas can be accessed.

2. The kernel runs a verifier on the bytecode to make sure the program is safe to run (`kernel/bpf/verifier.c`).

3. The kernel JIT compiles the bytecode to native code and inserts it in or attaches to the specified code location.

4. The inserted code writes data to ring buffers or generic key-value maps.

5. User-space programs (optionally) read the result values from the shared maps or ring buffers.

Differences between BPF and eBPF

As mentioned earlier, eBPF is an evolution of BPF. In the following section, we will talk about some of the specific changes and implementation details.

The primary differences between cBPF and eBPF VM implementations are their instruction set architecture, JIT compilation, and flexibility. eBPF provides a more powerful and flexible VM architecture, with a richer instruction set and a more efficient JIT compiler, making it a more versatile and powerful tool for packet filtering and other purposes. At a high level, some of the differences include:

-   **Instruction set**: BPF has a limited instruction set with only 12 instructions, while eBPF has a larger instruction set with over 30 instructions. The expanded instruction set in eBPF enables more complex filtering and other operations.

-   **Register size**: BPF uses 32-bit registers, while eBPF uses 64-bit registers. This means that eBPF can handle larger data structures and perform more complex operations.

-   **Program loading**: BPF programs can be loaded into the kernel in a limited way, only allowing the filter to be attached to a socket. On the other hand, eBPF programs can be attached to events in the kernel in more ways, such as through the **Traffic Control** (**TC**) subsystem, perf_events, and kprobes, allowing eBPF to be used for other purposes besides packet filtering.

-   **Security**: EBPF is designed with more safety features than BPF, including a two-stage verifier that checks the memory/kernel safety of the program before it is loaded into the kernel, and a sandbox that restricts access to certain kernel functions.

- **Compatibility**: EBPF is backwards compatible with BPF, which means that programs written for BPF can be executed on eBPF without modification. However, programs written for eBPF may not be compatible with BPF.

Overall, eBPF is a more modern and versatile packet filtering mechanism that offers better performance and safety than cBPF. However, cBPF is still widely used in many systems and can be a simpler and more lightweight option for basic packet filtering tasks. We will now look at some of these differences in detail.

Virtual machine

You may remember from *Chapter 1, Classic Berkeley Packet Filter*, cBPF uses a simple RISC architecture with a very limited set of instructions available (16 to be exact). These instructions were designed around filtering packets based on a simple set of criteria, that is, **tcp and ip**.

One of the primary differences between cBPF and eBPF is the virtual machine implementations, in particular, their **instruction set architecture (ISA)** as shown in *Table 2.1*:

Features	BPF implementation	eBPF implementation
Num of registers	2	10
Size of registers	32-bit (A, x)	64-bit registers (R0-R9)
Memory available	16 memory slots M0-15	512 bytes of stack space plus infinite map storage
Program Targets	Packets	Packets, kprobes, uprobes, tracepoints, sockets

Table 2.1: A comparison of BPF vs eBPF capabilities

With the initial eBPF commit, the VM original cBPF implementation evolved to become significantly more powerful. *Table 2.1* provides a comparison of the cBPF and eBPF VM capabilities.

eBPF has a more complex implementation, reusing the RISC architecture to allow the use of a wider range of instructions that will eventually be used for tracing security enforcement and networking mechanisms. You will see an expanded eBPF instruction set and a larger set of addressing modes (13 as compared to 9 in BPF) in *Table 2.2*:

Opcode	Addressing modes	Description
Ld	1, 2, 3, 4, 12	Load word into A
ldi	4	Load word into A
ldh	1, 2	Load half-word into A
ldb	1,2	Load byte into A
ldx	3, 4, 5, 12	Load word into X
ldxi	4	Load word into X
ldxb	5	Load byte into X
St	3	Store A into M[]
stx	3	Store X into M[]
Jmp	6	Jump to label
ja	6	Jump to label
jeq	7, 8, 9, 10	Jump on A == <x>
jneq	9, 10	Jump on A != <x>
jne	9, 10	Jump on A != <x>
jlt	9, 10	Jump on A < <x>
jle	9, 10	Jump on A <= <x>
jgt	7, 8, 9, 10	Jump on A > <x>
jge	7, 8, 9, 10	Jump on A >= <x>
jset	7, 8, 9, 10	Jump on A & <x>
add	0, 4	A + <x>
Sub	0, 4	A - <x>
mul	0, 4	A * <x>
Div	0, 4	A / <x>
mod	0, 4	A % <x>
neg	0, 4	!A
And	0, 4	A & <x>
or	0, 4	A	<x>
xor	0, 4	A ^ <x>
lsh	0, 4	A << <x>
rsh	0, 4	A >> <x>
Tax		Copy A into X
txa		Copy X into A
ret	4, 11	Return

Table 2.2: *eBPF instruction set*

eBPF has a larger set of addressing modes (13 of them) as compared to cBPF's 9 addressing modes. They are as follows:

Addressing mode	Syntax	Description
0	X/%x	Register X
1	[k]	BHW at byte offset k in the packet
2	[x + k]	BHW at the offset X + k in the packet
3	M[k]	Word at offset k in M[]
4	#k	Literal value stored in k
5	4*([k]&0xf)	Lower nibble * 4 at byte offset k in the packet
6	L	Jump label L
7	#k,Lt,Lf	Jump to Lt if true, otherwise jump to Lf
8	x/%x,Lt,Lf	Jump to Lt if true, otherwise jump to Lf
9	#k,Lt	Jump to Lt if predicate is true
10	x/%x,Lt	Jump to Lt if predicate is true
11	a/%a	Accumulator A
12	extension	BPF extension

Table 2.3: eBPF VM addressing modes

It is important to note that the instruction format has remained unchanged as shown in *Figure 1.7*.

eBPF verifier

The eBPF verifier helps to ensure the safety of the BPF program before it is compiled in the kernel. It does this in three steps:

1. Check the DAG to ensure that there are no loops or unreachable instructions.

2. Run a simulation of the program and perform a series of checks to ensure program validity. You can read more details in the BPF verifier documentation.

3. Ensure that the program has the capabilities (privileges) to run in the kernel.

eBPF JIT compiler

Once the eBPF program is verified, the JIT compiler compiles the program (see *Figure 2.2*). The kernel has a BPF JIT verifier that can compile BPF programs in 8 different CPU architectures (x86_64, SPARC, PowerPC, ARM, ARM64, MIPS, RISC-V and s390).

The compiler's general task is to take bytecode instructions and translate them to the specific instruction set required to run on the CPU architecture:

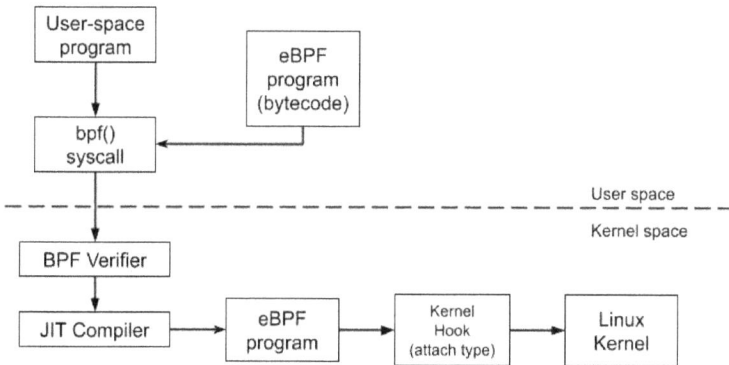

Figure 2.2: The eBPF program verification and compilation process

Both the verifier and compiler run in kernel space and is invoked whenever a program is about to be loaded into the kernel.

eBPF helpers

eBPF helpers are special functions available within eBPF programs. There are over 140 different functions currently available that assist in reading/writing from maps, extracting data from socket buffers, printing data to user space, and a multitude of helpful macros. We will cover this in detail in *Chapter 3, eBPF Programming Concepts*.

You can find the man page for the helpers here bpf-helpers(7).

eBPF maps

Maps are a means to provide generic storage that can be read from and written to from both kernel and user-space. 33 different map types are available which can store a variety of different kernel structures and datatypes.

A map is defined by the following properties:

- Type
- Max number of elements
- Key size in bytes
- Value size in bytes

For example:

```
struct {
__uint(type, BPF_MAP_TYPE_ARRAY);
__type(key, u32);
__type(value, u64);
__uint(max_entries, 100);
} my_map SEC(".maps");
```

This creates a map called **my_map** which is an array. The key size is an unsigned 32-bit integer, and the possible values are an unsigned 64-bit integer. It allows **100** entries to be created.

We will discuss the different eBPF map types and how to store and retrieve data from them in *Chapter 3, eBPF Programming Concepts.*

Conclusion

The evolution of cBPF to iBPF to eBPF has created a new powerful mechanism in Linux to write low-level efficient in-kernel programs. The use of eBPF has largely made kernel modules obsolete. EBPF provides an upgraded VM with significantly more capabilities than its cBPF predecessor.

eBPF has a wide range of use cases in modern computing systems, including system tracing and analysis, network security, performance optimization, containerization, and compliance monitoring. It provides several key benefits to developers and system administrators, including real-time monitoring and analysis, improved system performance and security, compliance monitoring, cross-platform compatibility, reduced development time, and a safe execution environment.

In the following chapters, we will explore the programming concepts around eBPF and then deep-dive into observability, networking, and security uses of eBPF. Finally, we will discuss productionalizing eBPF programs in your environment.

CHAPTER 3

eBPF Programming Concepts

Introduction

In *Chapter 1, Classic Berkeley Packet Filter*, we looked at two applications of cBPF programs, Linux Socket Filter and seccomp-BPF programs. These filters were applied using the **setsockopt** and **prctl** functions. eBPF has a much larger set of programming primitives than its cBPF counterpart, which we will explore in this chapter.

eBPF programming is centered around a few key concepts: the **bpf(2)** system call, BPF program types, BPF maps, and BPF helper functions. In this chapter, we will explain each in detail. Refer to the following figure:

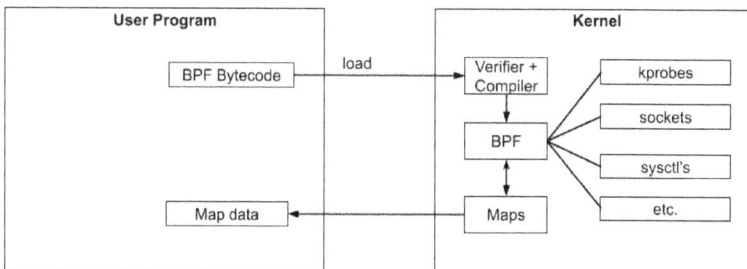

Figure 3.1: The eBPF subsystem

Structure

This chapter covers the following topics:

- bpf() system call
- eBPF program types
- BPF attach types
- Map types
- Map-specific helpers
- Other BPF helpers
- Program arguments
- Loops
- Tail calls
- Sleepable programs
- Program return codes
- bpftool

Objectives

By the end of this chapter, you will understand all the primitives involved in writing eBPF programs. You will learn how user-space interacts with kernel space and understand all the eBPF program, attachment, and map types available for you to use. You will also understand some of the intricacies of eBPF programs and their limitations.

bpf() system call

In cBPF, we attached BPF filters using the **setsockopt()** and **prctl()** functions. In eBPF, we use the **bpf()** system call to interact with eBPF from user-space.

bpf(2) system call is defined in the following way:

```
include <linux/bpf.h>
int bpf(int cmd, union bpf_attr *attr, unsigned int size);
```

Note: It is possible that the contents of the man page are not consistent with the configuration/functionality of your machine.

The **bpf(2)** system call was first defined in Linux 3.18 *Alexei Starovoitov's* commit. You can find the system calls current implementation in **kernel/bpf/syscall.c**.

Let us dissect the arguments.

int cmd

The **cmd** argument outlines what operation the system call should be taking. In **bpf.h**, the **enum bpf_cmd** defines the list of possible operations:

Note: As of kernel 6.3, there are 36 commands you can send to the BPF system calls. We will not cover them all in this book. They are defined in include/uapi/linux/bpf.h.

```
enum bpf_cmd {
        BPF_MAP_CREATE,
        BPF_MAP_LOOKUP_ELEM,
        BPF_MAP_UPDATE_ELEM,
        BPF_MAP_DELETE_ELEM,
        BPF_MAP_GET_NEXT_KEY,
        BPF_PROG_LOAD,
        BPF_OBJ_PIN,
        BPF_OBJ_GET,
        BPF_PROG_ATTACH,
        BPF_PROG_DETACH,
        BPF_PROG_TEST_RUN,
        BPF_PROG_GET_NEXT_ID,
        BPF_MAP_GET_NEXT_ID,
        BPF_PROG_GET_FD_BY_ID,
        BPF_MAP_GET_FD_BY_ID,
        BPF_OBJ_GET_INFO_BY_FD,
        BPF_PROG_QUERY,
        BPF_RAW_TRACEPOINT_OPEN,
        BPF_BTF_LOAD,
        BPF_BTF_GET_FD_BY_ID,
        BPF_TASK_FD_QUERY,
        BPF_MAP_LOOKUP_AND_DELETE_ELEM,
        BPF_MAP_FREEZE,
```

```
BPF_BTF_GET_NEXT_ID,
BPF_MAP_LOOKUP_BATCH,
BPF_MAP_LOOKUP_AND_DELETE_BATCH,
BPF_MAP_UPDATE_BATCH,
BPF_MAP_DELETE_BATCH,
BPF_LINK_CREATE,
BPF_LINK_UPDATE,
BPF_LINK_GET_FD_BY_ID,
BPF_LINK_GET_NEXT_ID,
BPF_ENABLE_STATS,
BPF_ITER_CREATE,
BPF_LINK_DETACH,
BPF_PROG_BIND_MAP,
}
```

Here is a summary of what each command type does:

- **BPF_MAP_CREATE**: Create a map and return a file descriptor that refers to the map.

- **BPF_MAP_LOOKUP_ELEM**: Look up an element with a given key in the map referred to by the file descriptor **map_fd**.

- **BPF_MAP_UPDATE_ELEM**: Create or update an element (key/value pair) in a specified map.

- **BPF_MAP_DELETE_ELEM**: Look up and delete an element by key in a specified map.

- **BPF_MAP_GET_NEXT_KEY**: Look up an element by key in a specified map and return the key of the next element. It can be used to iterate over all elements in the map.

- **BPF_PROG_LOAD**: Verify and load an eBPF program, returning a new file descriptor associated with the program.

- **BPF_OBJ_PIN**: Pin an eBPF program or map referred by the specified **bpf_fd** to the provided **pathname** on the filesystem.

- **BPF_OBJ_GET**: Obtain information about the eBPF object corresponding to **bpf_fd**.

- **BPF_PROG_ATTACH**: Attach an eBPF program to a **target_fd** at the specified **attach_type** hook.

- **BPF_PROG_DETACH**: Detach the eBPF program associated with the **target_fd** at the hook specified by **attach_type**. The program must have been previously attached using **BPF_PROG_ATTACH**.

- **BPF_PROG_TEST_RUN**: Run the eBPF program associated with the **prog_fd** a **specific** number of times (as defined in the **bpf_attr** argument).

- **BPF_PROG_GET_NEXT_ID**: Fetch the next eBPF program currently loaded into the kernel.

- **BPF_MAP_GET_NEXT_ID**: Fetch the next eBPF map currently loaded into the kernel.

- **BPF_PROG_GET_FD_BY_ID**: Open a file descriptor for the eBPF program corresponding to **prog_id**.

- **BPF_MAP_GET_FD_BY_ID**: Open a file descriptor for the eBPF map corresponding to **map_id**.

- **BPF_OBJ_GET_INFO_BY_FD**: Obtain information about the eBPF object corresponding to **bpf_fd**.

- **BPF_PROG_QUERY**: Obtain information about eBPF programs associated with the specified **attach_type** hook.

- **BPF_RAW_TRACEPOINT_OPEN**: Attach an eBPF program to a tracepoint **name** to access kernel internal arguments of the tracepoint in their raw form.

- **BPF_BTF_LOAD**: Verify and load **BPF Type Format** (BTF) metadata into the kernel, returning a new file descriptor associated with the metadata.

- **BPF_BTF_GET_FD_BY_ID**: Open a file descriptor for the BTF corresponding to **btf_id**.

- **BPF_TASK_FD_QUERY**: Obtain information about eBPF programs associated with the target process identified by **pid** and **fd**.

- **BPF_MAP_LOOKUP_AND_DELETE_ELEM**: Look up an element with the given **key** in the map referred to by the file descriptor **fd**, and if found, delete the element.

- **BPF_MAP_FREEZE**: Freeze the permissions of the specified map.

- **BPF_BTF_GET_NEXT_ID**: Fetch the next BTF object currently loaded into the kernel.

- **BPF_MAP_LOOKUP_BATCH**: Iterate and fetch multiple elements in a map.

- **BPF_MAP_LOOKUP_AND_DELETE_BATCH**: Iterate and delete all elements in a map.

- **BPF_MAP_UPDATE_BATCH**: Update multiple elements in a map by **key**.

- **BPF_MAP_DELETE_BATCH**: Delete multiple elements in a map by **key**.

- **BPF_LINK_CREATE**: Attach an eBPF program to a **target_fd** at the specified **attach_type** hook and return a file descriptor handle for managing the link.

- **BPF_LINK_UPDATE**: Update the eBPF program in the specified **link_fd** to **new_prog_fd**.

- **BPF_LINK_GET_FD_BY_ID**: Open a file descriptor for the eBPF link corresponding to **link_id**.

- **BPF_LINK_GET_NEXT_ID**: Fetch the next eBPF link currently loaded into the kernel.

- **BPF_ENABLE_STATS**: Enable eBPF runtime statistics gathering.

- **BPF_ITER_CREATE**: Create an iterator on top of the specified **link_fd** (as previously created using **BPF_LINK_CREATE**) and return a file descriptor that can be used to trigger the iteration.

- **BPF_LINK_DETACH**: Forcefully detach the specified **link_fd** from its corresponding attachment point.

- **BPF_PROG_BIND_MAP**: Bind a map to the lifetime of an eBPF program.

union bpf_attr *attr

This argument is used to pass in a **struct** that contains metadata about your command. As shown in the following code example, the struct used for the **BPF_MAP_CREATE** command has 4 required parameters (not shown here) and 14 extra parameters:

```
struct { /* anonymous struct used by BPF_MAP_CREATE command
*/
        __u32   map_type;   /* one of enum bpf_map_type */
        __u32   key_size;   /* size of key in bytes */
        __u32   value_size; /* size of value in bytes */
        __u32   max_entries;    /* max number of entries in
a map */
        __u32   map_flags;  /* BPF_MAP_CREATE related
                     * flags defined above.
                     */
        __u32   inner_map_fd;   /* fd pointing to the inner
map */
        __u32   numa_node;  /* numa node (effective only if
                     * BPF_F_NUMA_NODE is set).
                     */
        char    map_name[BPF_OBJ_NAME_LEN];
        __u32   map_ifindex;    /* ifindex of netdev to
create on */
        __u32   btf_fd;     /* fd pointing to a BTF type
data */
        __u32   btf_key_type_id;    /* BTF type_id of the
key */
        __u32   btf_value_type_id;  /* BTF type_id of the
value */
        __u32   btf_vmlinux_value_type_id;/* BTF type_id of
a kernel-
                        * struct stored as the
                        * map value
                        */     __u64   map_extra;
    };
```

Each of the different **struct** types are listed in Appendix C.

unsigned int size

The size argument is the size of the union pointed to by **attr**.

Return values

The **bpf()** system call has some generic error codes that may be returned when the system call is executed. They are as follows:

- **BPF_MAP_CREATE**: The new file descriptor associated with the eBPF map.

- **BPF_PROG_LOAD**: The new file descriptor associated with the eBPF program.

- **All other commands**: 0.

On error, **-1** is returned, and **errno** is set to indicate the error.

Error numbers

If the **bpf(2)** system call returns an error, the following error numbers are returned:

- **-EPERM (-14)**: Does not have capability privileges.

- **-E2BIG (-7)**: Size of the **bpf_attr** is too large.

- **-EFAULT (-14)**: Attributes cannot be copied from user-space.

- **EACCES**: For **BPF_PROG_LOAD**, even though all program instructions are valid, the program has been rejected because it was deemed unsafe by the BPF verifier.

- **EINVAL**: The value specified in **cmd** is not recognized by this kernel.

- For **BPF_MAP_CREATE**, either **map_type** or attributes are invalid.

- **For BPF_MAP_*_ELEM** commands, some of the fields of **union bpf_attr** are:

  - For **BPF_PROG_LOAD**, indicates an attempt to load an invalid program. eBPF programs can be deemed invalid due to unrecognized instructions, the use of reserved fields, jumps out of range, infinite loops or calls of unknown functions.

- **ENOENT**: For **BPF_MAP_LOOKUP_ELEM** or **BPF_MAP_DELETE_ELEM**, indicates that the element with the given key was not found.

- **ENOMEM**: Cannot allocate sufficient memory.

There are more specific error codes for each map type, which are in Appendix D.

eBPF program types

The eBPF program type **prog_type** determines the subset of kernel helper functions that the program may call. The program type also determines the program input (context)—the format of **struct bpf_context** (which is the data structure passed into the eBPF program as the first argument — which is intentionally undefined in the kernel).

For example, a tracing program does not have access to the exact same subset of helper functions as a socket filter program (though they may have some helpers in common). Similarly, the input (context) for a tracing program is a set of register values, while for a socket filter, it is a **socket buffer** (**SKB**). The access you get to the system will depend on the program type selected.

While this book attempts to categorize program types by their main use (observability/tracing, networking, and security), there is no formal definition or source of truth for these program types.

In the **bpf.h** Linux kernel file, under the **enum bpf_prog_type**, a set of BPF program types is given in the following:

```
$ grep BPF_PROG_TYPE linux/include/uapi/linux/bpf.h
enum bpf_prog_type {
        BPF_PROG_TYPE_UNSPEC,
        BPF_PROG_TYPE_SOCKET_FILTER,
        BPF_PROG_TYPE_KPROBE,
        BPF_PROG_TYPE_SCHED_CLS,
        BPF_PROG_TYPE_SCHED_ACT,
        BPF_PROG_TYPE_TRACEPOINT,
        BPF_PROG_TYPE_XDP,
        BPF_PROG_TYPE_PERF_EVENT,
        BPF_PROG_TYPE_CGROUP_SKB,
        BPF_PROG_TYPE_CGROUP_SOCK,
        BPF_PROG_TYPE_LWT_IN,
        BPF_PROG_TYPE_LWT_OUT,
        BPF_PROG_TYPE_LWT_XMIT,
        BPF_PROG_TYPE_SOCK_OPS,
        BPF_PROG_TYPE_SK_SKB,
        BPF_PROG_TYPE_CGROUP_DEVICE,
        BPF_PROG_TYPE_SK_MSG,
```

```
    BPF_PROG_TYPE_RAW_TRACEPOINT,
    BPF_PROG_TYPE_CGROUP_SOCK_ADDR,
    BPF_PROG_TYPE_LWT_SEG6LOCAL,
    BPF_PROG_TYPE_LIRC_MODE2,
    BPF_PROG_TYPE_SK_REUSEPORT,
    BPF_PROG_TYPE_FLOW_DISSECTOR,
    BPF_PROG_TYPE_CGROUP_SYSCTL,
    BPF_PROG_TYPE_RAW_TRACEPOINT_WRITABLE,
    BPF_PROG_TYPE_CGROUP_SOCKOPT,
    BPF_PROG_TYPE_TRACING,
    BPF_PROG_TYPE_STRUCT_OPS,
    BPF_PROG_TYPE_EXT,
    BPF_PROG_TYPE_LSM,
    BPF_PROG_TYPE_SK_LOOKUP,
    BPF_PROG_TYPE_SYSCALL,
};
```

Depending on your distribution and kernel version, you may or may not have all the program-types available by default. Each of the eBPF program-types can be enabled via different kernel config parameters. We will now list each kernel configuration parameter that needs to be set to **y** to enable the corresponding set of programs:

- **CONFIG_NET=y**

  - **BPF_PROG_TYPE_SOCKET_FILTER**: A network packet filter. This provides the same functionality as cBPF packet filters.

  - **BPF_PROG_TYPE_SCHED_CLS**: A network Traffic Control classifier.

  - **BPF_PROG_TYPE_SCHED_ACT**: A network TC action program.

  - **BPF_PROG_TYPE_XDP**: A network packet filter run from the device-driver receive path.

  - **BPF_PROG_TYPE_LWT_IN/ BPF_PROG_TYPE_ LWT_OUT/ BPF_PROG_TYPE_LWT_XMIT/ BPF_ PROG_TYPE_LWT_SEG6LOCAL**: A network packet filter for lightweight tunnels.

- o **BPF_PROG_TYPE_SOCK_OPS**: A program for setting socket parameters.

- o **BPF_PROG_TYPE_SK_SKB**: A network packet filter for forwarding packets between sockets.

- o **BPF_PROG_TYPE_SK_MSG**: Controls whether a message sent to a socket should be delivered.

- o **BPF_PROG_TYPE_FLOW_DISSECTOR**: BPF flow dissector is an attempt to reimplement C-based flow dissector logic in BPF to gain all the benefits of BPF verifier (namely, limits on the number of instructions and tail calls).

- **CONFIG_CGROUP_BPF=y and CONFIG_NET=y**

  - o **BPF_PROG_TYPE_CGROUP_SKB**: A network packet filter for control groups.

  - o **BPF_PROG_TYPE_CGROUP_SOCK**: A network packet filter for control groups that are allowed to modify socket options.

  - o **BPF_PROG_TYPE_CGROUP_SOCK_ADDR**: Allows you to manipulate the IP addresses and port numbers that user-space programs are attached to when they are controlled by specific cgroups.

- **CONFIG_BPF_EVENTS=y**

  - o **BPF_PROG_TYPE_KPROBE**: Attach a program to a **kernel probe (Kprobe)**.

  - o **BPF_PROG_TYPE_TRACEPOINT**: Determine whether a tracepoint should fire or not.

  - o **BPF_PROG_TYPE_PERF_EVENT**: Determine whether a perf event handler should fire or not.

  - o **BPF_PROG_TYPE_RAW_TRACEPOINT**: Access kernel internal arguments of the tracepoints in their raw form.

  - o **BPF_PROG_TYPE_RAW_TRACEPOINT_WRITABLE**: Determine whether a tracepoint should fire and write to a buffer.

- o **BPF_PROG_TYPE_TRACING**: Highly efficient tracing, a successor to **BPF_PROG_TYPE_KPROBE**.

- **CONFIG_CGROUP_BPF=y**

  - o **BPF_PROG_TYPE_CGROUP_DEVICE**: An access filter to host devices for cgroup v2.

  - o **BPF_PROG_TYPE_CGROUP_SYSCTL**: The hook has to be attached to a cgroup and will be called every time a process inside that cgroup tries to read from or write to sysctl parameter.

  - o **BPF_PROG_TYPE_CGROUP_SOCKOPT**: This is triggered before/after the kernel handing of sockopt.

- **CONFIG_BPF_LIRC_MODE2=y**

  - o **BPF_PROG_TYPE_LIRC_MODE2**: These eBPF programs can be used to decode IR into scancodes, for IR protocols not supported by the kernel decoders. We will not cover this program type.

- **CONFIG_INET=y**

  - o **BPF_PROG_TYPE_SK_REUSEPORT**: It allows you to write BPF programs that hook into the logic that the kernel uses to decide whether it is going to reuse a port.

  - o **BPF_PROG_TYPE_SK_LOOKUP**

- **CONFIG_BPF_JIT=y**

  - o **BPF_PROG_TYPE_STRUCT_OPT**: It is an infra to allow implementing some specific kernel's function pointers in BPF.

  - o **BPF_PROG_TYPE_EXT**: The **BPF_PROG_TYPE_EXT** program type is a placeholder. The extension program can call the same bpf helper functions as the target program. Single **BPF_PROG_TYPE_EXT** type is used to extend XDP, SKB, and all other program types.

- **CONFIG_BPF_JIT=y and CONFIG_BPF_LSM=y**

  - o **BPF_PROG_TYPE_LSM**: BPF programs that can be attached to **Linux Security Module (LSM)** hooks.

- **CONFIG_NETFILTER_BPF_LINK=y**

  o **BPF_PROG_TYPE_NETFILTER**: Allows you to attach network filtering rules (BPF programs) to the nftables processing flows.

  Enabled by default, no changes required.

  o **BPF_PROG_TYPE_SYSTEM CALL**: A program that has the ability to call **sys_bpf** and **sys_close** system calls.

BPF attach types

In *Chapter 2, Extended Berkeley Packet Filter*, we briefly mentioned BPF attach types. Attach types define where the eBPF program gets attached to the kernel (that is, what kernel action triggers the eBPF program to run) and what helper functions are available to the program. At the time of writing, there are more than 40 attachment types defined in **include/uapi/linux/bpf.h** seen in the following code example:

```
enum bpf_attach_type {
    BPF_CGROUP_INET_INGRESS,
    BPF_CGROUP_INET_EGRESS,
    BPF_CGROUP_INET_SOCK_CREATE,
    BPF_CGROUP_SOCK_OPS,
    BPF_SK_SKB_STREAM_PARSER,
    BPF_SK_SKB_STREAM_VERDICT,
    BPF_CGROUP_DEVICE,
    BPF_SK_MSG_VERDICT,
    BPF_CGROUP_INET4_BIND,
    BPF_CGROUP_INET6_BIND,
    BPF_CGROUP_INET4_CONNECT,
    BPF_CGROUP_INET6_CONNECT,
    BPF_CGROUP_INET4_POST_BIND,
    BPF_CGROUP_INET6_POST_BIND,
    BPF_CGROUP_UDP4_SENDMSG,
    BPF_CGROUP_UDP6_SENDMSG,
    BPF_LIRC_MODE2,
    BPF_FLOW_DISSECTOR,
    BPF_CGROUP_SYSCTL,
```

```
    BPF_CGROUP_UDP4_RECVMSG,
    BPF_CGROUP_UDP6_RECVMSG,
    BPF_CGROUP_GETSOCKOPT,
    BPF_CGROUP_SETSOCKOPT,
    BPF_TRACE_RAW_TP,
    BPF_TRACE_FENTRY,
    BPF_TRACE_FEXIT,
    BPF_MODIFY_RETURN,
    BPF_LSM_MAC,
    BPF_TRACE_ITER,
    BPF_CGROUP_INET4_GETPEERNAME,
    BPF_CGROUP_INET6_GETPEERNAME,
    BPF_CGROUP_INET4_GETSOCKNAME,
    BPF_CGROUP_INET6_GETSOCKNAME,
    BPF_XDP_DEVMAP,
    BPF_CGROUP_INET_SOCK_RELEASE,
    BPF_XDP_CPUMAP,
    BPF_SK_LOOKUP,
    BPF_XDP,
    BPF_SK_SKB_VERDICT,
    BPF_SK_REUSEPORT_SELECT,
    BPF_SK_REUSEPORT_SELECT_OR_MIGRATE,
    BPF_PERF_EVENT,
    BPF_TRACE_KPROBE_MULTI,
    BPF_LSM_CGROUP,
    __MAX_BPF_ATTACH_TYPE
};
```

You will notice that there are a lot of **BPF_CGROUP_INET_*** types of attachments. This is because the **BPF_PROG_TYPE_CGROUP_SOCK** and **BPF_PROG_TYPE_CGROUP_SOCK_ADDR** program types can be attached to different network events (e.g. **bind**, **connect**, **post_bind**), but use the same program type.

In some cases, there is an implicit correlation between program type and attachment type, **BPF_PROG_TYPE_SOCKET_FILTER** where the attachment type does not have to be explicitly defined as there is a one-to-one mapping of hooks to programs. This kernel documentation page lists the attached types for each program type as well as the ELF

Section name that you need to specify to invoke the program (more on that in *Chapter 4, eBPF Programming Libraries and Frameworks*). We have also provided a copy in Appendix A.

In Appendix A, you will notice the column called ELF Section Name. This is used at the top of your BPF program to indicate what type of kernel action you want to attach your eBPF program to. You can see the **xdp** attach type in the following code example:

```
SEC(«xdp")
int xsk_redir_prog(struct xdp_md *ctx)
{
    __u32 index = ctx->rx_queue_index;

    if (bpf_map_lookup_elem(&xsks_map, &index))
        return bpf_redirect_map(&xsks_map, index, 0);
    return XDP_PASS;
}
```

As we discuss each program type in *Chapter 7, eBPF Observability, Chapter 8, eBPF Networking*, and *Chapter 9, eBPF Security*, we will discuss the attached types for each BPF program type in more detail.

Map types

As mentioned earlier, eBPF allows data storage (within the program) and communication of data between kernel-space and user-space. This is achieved by utilizing eBPF maps. eBPF maps are key-value stores that reside in memory. They can be accessed by any BPF program that knows about them and be read/ written to via file-descriptors in user-space.

Like variables in traditional programming, eBPF maps can store various datatypes in an efficient manner. Some map types are optimized for storing data on a per-CPU basis. The eBPF verifier has mechanisms to ensure that maps are accessed safely, avoiding both kernel and application crashes. Supported map types are declared in **bpf.h**:

```
$ grep bpf_map_type linux/include/uapi/linux/bpf.h
enum bpf_map_type {
        BPF_MAP_TYPE_UNSPEC,
        BPF_MAP_TYPE_HASH,
        BPF_MAP_TYPE_ARRAY,
```

```
    BPF_MAP_TYPE_PROG_ARRAY,
    BPF_MAP_TYPE_PERF_EVENT_ARRAY,
    BPF_MAP_TYPE_PERCPU_HASH,
    BPF_MAP_TYPE_PERCPU_ARRAY,
    BPF_MAP_TYPE_STACK_TRACE,
    BPF_MAP_TYPE_CGROUP_ARRAY,
    BPF_MAP_TYPE_LRU_HASH,
    BPF_MAP_TYPE_LRU_PERCPU_HASH,
    BPF_MAP_TYPE_LPM_TRIE,
    BPF_MAP_TYPE_ARRAY_OF_MAPS,
    BPF_MAP_TYPE_HASH_OF_MAPS,
    BPF_MAP_TYPE_DEVMAP,
    BPF_MAP_TYPE_SOCKMAP,
    BPF_MAP_TYPE_CPUMAP,
    BPF_MAP_TYPE_XSKMAP,
    BPF_MAP_TYPE_SOCKHASH,
    BPF_MAP_TYPE_CGROUP_STORAGE,
    BPF_MAP_TYPE_REUSEPORT_SOCKARRAY,
    BPF_MAP_TYPE_PERCPU_CGROUP_STORAGE,
    BPF_MAP_TYPE_QUEUE,
    BPF_MAP_TYPE_STACK,
   BPF_MAP_TYPE_SK_STORAGE,
    BPF_MAP_TYPE_DEVMAP_HASH,
   BPF_MAP_TYPE_STRUCT_OPS,
   BPF_MAP_TYPE_RINGBUF,
   BPF_MAP_TYPE_INODE_STORAGE,
   BPF_MAP_TYPE_TASK_STORAGE,
   BPF_MAP_TYPE_BLOOM_FILTER,
   BPF_MAP_TYPE_USER_RINGBUF,
   BPF_MAP_TYPE_CGROUP_STORAGE,
};
```

A basic example of using maps can be found in example 5.2. Further documentation for most of the map types can be found at: **https://docs. kernel.org/next/bpf/maps.html**.

BPF_MAP_TYPE_HASH

Description: A hash table map. Hash lookup matches the key to the appropriate value via a hashing function rather than an indexed lookup. Unlike the array case, values can be deleted from a hash map. Hash maps are ideal when using a value such as an IP address for storage/retrieval.

Introduced: 3.19

BPF_MAP_TYPE_ARRAY

Description: An array of elements. The key is the array index, and elements cannot be deleted.

Introduced: 3.19

BPF_MAP_TYPE_PROG_ARRAY

Description: An array of file descriptions corresponding to other eBPF programs. An array of BPF programs is used as a jump table by **bpf_tail_call()**.

Introduced: 4.2

BPF_MAP_TYPE_PERF_EVENT_ARRAY

Description: Stores pointers to **perf_event**. Array map which is used by the kernel in **bpf_perf_event_output()** to associate tracing output with a specific key. User-space programs associate **file descriptors** (**fds**) with each key, and can **poll()** those fds to receive notification that data has been traced.

Introduced: 4.3

BPF_MAP_TYPE_PERCPU_HASH

Description: A hash table map maintained on a per CPU basis.

Introduced: 4.6

BPF_MAP_TYPE_PERCPU_ARRAY

Description: An array maintained on a per CPU basis.

Introduced: 4.6

BPF_MAP_TYPE_STACK_TRACE

Description: Storage for stack traces. defined in **kernel/bpf/ stackmap.c**. Kernel programs can store stacks via the **bpf_get_ stackid()** helper.

Introduced: 4.6

BPF_MAP_TYPE_CGROUP_ARRAY

Description: Stores pointers to control groups. Array map used to store cgroup fds in user-space for later use in BPF programs which call **bpf_skb_under_cgroup()** to check if **socket buffer** (**skb**) is associated with the cgroup in the cgroup array at the specified index.

Introduced: 4.8

BPF_MAP_TYPE_LRU_HASH

Description: A hash table that only retains the most recently used items. Each hash maintains an **least recently used** (**LRU**) list for each bucket to inform delete when the hash bucket fills up.

Introduced: 4.10

BPF_MAP_TYPE_LRU_PERCPU_ HASH

Description: A per CPU hash table that only retains the most recently used items

Introduced: 4.10

BPF_MAP_TYPE_LPM_TRIE

Description: A longest prefix match trie, good for matching IP addresses. Map supporting efficient longest prefix matching. Useful for storage/retrieval of IP routes for example.

Introduced: 4.11

BPF_MAP_TYPE_ARRAY_OF_MAPS

Description: A map-in-map data structure. Allows map-in-map definition where the values are the file descriptors for the inner maps.

Only two levels of map are supported, i.e. a map containing maps, not a map containing maps containing maps. **BPF_MAP_TYPE_PROG_ARRAY** does not support map-in-map functionality as it would make tail call verification harder.

Introduced: 4.12

BPF_MAP_TYPE_HASH_OF_MAPS

Description: A map-in-map data structure. Similar to **ARRAY_OF_MAPS** for hash maps.

Introduced: 4.12

BPF_MAP_TYPE_DEVMAP

Description: It is used for storing and looking up network device references. It performs a similar role to sockmap, with net devices for XDP and **bpf_redirect()**.

Introduced: 4.14

BPF_MAP_TYPE_SOCKMAP

Description: Stores and looks up sockets and allows socket redirection with BPF helper functions. Sockmaps are used primarily for socket redirection, where sockets are added to a socket map and referenced by a key that dictates redirection when **bpf_sockmap_redirect()** is called.

Introduced: 4.14

BPF_MAP_TYPE_CPUMAP

Description: The CPUMAP represents the CPUs in the system indexed as the map-key, and the map-value is the config setting (per CPUMAP entry). Each CPUMAP entry has a dedicated kernel thread bound to the given CPU to represent the remote CPU execution unit.

Introduced: 4.15

BPF_MAP_TYPE_XSKMAP

Description: A map that stores references to open **AF_XDP** sockets.

Introduced: 4.18

BPF_MAP_TYPE_SOCKHASH

Description: Similar to **BPF_MAP_TYPE_SOCKMAP** but uses a hash table instead.

Introduced: 4.18

BPF_MAP_TYPE_CGROUP_ STORAGE

Description: A hash table map for BPF programs running in cgroups.

Introduced: 4.19

BPF_MAP_TYPE_REUSEPORT_ SOCKARRAY

Description: These maps are mainly used with **BPF_PROG_TYPE_SK_ REUSEPORT** program types. Combined, they give you control to decide how to filter and serve incoming packets from the network device.

Introduced: 4.19

BPF_MAP_TYPE_PERCPU_CGROUP_ STORAGE

Description: The map provides local storage in the cgroup that the BPF program is attached to. It provides faster and simpler access than the general-purpose hash table, which performs a hash table lookups, and requires users to track live cgroups on their own.

Introduced: 4.20

BPF_MAP_TYPE_QUEUE

Description: A **first-in, first-out** (**FIFO**) element queue.

Introduced: 4.20

BPF_MAP_TYPE_STACK

Description: A **last-in, first-out** (**LIFO**) element storage.

Introduced: 4.20

BPF_MAP_TYPE_SK_STORAGE

Description: A hash map to storage sockets utilized by a BPF program.

Introduced: 5.2

BPF_MAP_TYPE_DEVMAP_HASH

Description: Lookup devices by a hashed index. This allows maps to be densely packed, so they can be smaller.

Introduced: 5.4

BPF_MAP_TYPE_STRUCT_OPS

Description: Allows storing some specific kernel's function pointers in BPF.

Introduced: 5.6

BPF_MAP_TYPE_RINGBUF

Description: A simple circular (ring) buffer. The size of the ring buffer has to be a power of 2 value.

Introduced: 5.8

BPF_MAP_TYPE_INODE_STORAGE

Description: The map that can store references to inodes. The lifecycle of the storage is managed with the life cycle of the inode (i.e. the storage is destroyed along with the owning inode)

Introduced: 5.4

BPF_MAP_TYPE_TASK_STORAGE

Description: Similar to storage for sockets and inodes, this allows for storage of **task_struct**. The life-cycle of storage is managed with the life cycle of the **task_struct** (i.e. the storage is destroyed along with the owning task with a callback to the **bpf_task_storage_free()** from the **task_free** LSM hook).

Introduced: 5.11

BPF_MAP_TYPE_BLOOM_FILTER

Description: Allows the creation of a Bloom filter. The Bloom filter map does not have keys, only values.

Introduced: 5.16

BPF_MAP_TYPE_USER_RINGBUF

Description: Similar in structure to **BPF_MAP_TYPE_RINGBUF**, this allows user-space BPF programs to produce entries into the **RINGBUF** to be consumed by the kernel-space BPF program.

Introduced: 6.1

Map-specific helpers

The eBPF ecosystem provides helper-functions, known simply as helpers, in order to perform **create, read, update, delete** (**CRUD**) operations on eBPF maps. User-space map interactions are done via the **BPF()** system call.

You can find these functions in **tools/lib/bpf/bpf.c**. The documentation for these functions can be found in the **bpf-helpers(7)** man-page:

```
int bpf_create_map(enum bpf_map_type map_type, int key_
size, int value_size, int max_entries, u32 map_flags)
```

- **Description**: Create a BPF map of the specified type, with key/value size, of **max_entries** size with map flags specified.

- **Returns**: File descriptor for map on success, negative error on failure.

```
int bpf_create_map_node(enum bpf_map_type map_type, int
key_size, int value_size, int max_entries, u32 map_flags,
int node)
```

- **Description**: NUMA node-specific creation of BPF map.

- **Returns**: File descriptor for map on success, negative error on failure.

```
int bpf_create_map_in_map(enum bpf_map_type map_type, int
key_size, int inner_map_fd, int max_entries, u32 map_flags)
```

- **Description**: Create a map of the specified type, passing in fd of the inner map as a representative

- **Returns**: File descriptor for map on success, negative error on failure.

```
int bpf_create_map_in_map_node(enum bpf_map_type map_type,
int key_size, int inner_map_fd, int max_entries, u32 map_
flags, int node)
```

- **Description**: NUMA node-specific creation of BPF map-in-map.

- **Returns**: File descriptor for map on success, negative error on failure.

```
int bpf_map_update_elem(int fd, const void *key, const
void *value, u64 flags)
```

- **Description**: Update element with specified key with new value.

Other BPF helpers

eBPF currently contains 211 helper functions that can be used in eBPF programs. The helpers available for you to use will depend on the eBPF program type you are using. For example, BPF programs that are attached to network sockets have access to a different set of helper functions than BPF programs attached to kernel kprobes. In **kernel/bpf/helpers.c**, the **const struct bpf_func_proto *bpf_base_func_proto(enum bpf_func_id func_id)** function defines the base eBPF helpers that are available to every program type. At the time of this writing, there are 55 base functions available.

It would be exhaustive to list the helpers available per program type in this chapter, so instead we will link you to the location that they are defined in the kernel:

- **BPF_PROG_TYPE_SOCKET_FILTER**: **net/core/filter.c**

- **BPF_PROG_TYPE_KPROBE**: **kernel/tracing/bpf_trace.c**

- **BPF_PROG_TYPE_SCHED_CLS**: **net/core/filter.c**

- **BPF_PROG_TYPE_SCHED_ACT**: **net/core/filter.c**

- **BPF_PROG_TYPE_TRACEPOINT**: **kernel/tracing/bpf_trace.c**

- **BPF_PROG_TYPE_XDP**: **net/core/filter.c**

- BPF_PROG_TYPE_PERF_EVENT: kernel/tracing/bpf_trace.c

- BPF_PROG_TYPE_CGROUP_SKB: net/core/filter.c

- BPF_PROG_TYPE_CGROUP_SOCK: net/core/filter.c

- BPF_PROG_TYPE_LWT_IN: net/core/filter.c

- BPF_PROG_TYPE_LWT_OUT: net/core/filter.c

- BPF_PROG_TYPE_LWT_XMIT: net/core/filter.c

- BPF_PROG_TYPE_SOCK_OPS: net/core/filter.c

- BPF_PROG_TYPE_SK_SKB: net/core/filter.c

- BPF_PROG_TYPE_CGROUP_DEVICE: kernel/bpf/cgroup.c

- BPF_PROG_TYPE_SK_MSG: net/core/filter.c

- BPF_PROG_TYPE_RAW_TRACEPOINT: kernel/tracing/bpf_trace.c

- BPF_PROG_TYPE_CGROUP_SOCK_ADDR: net/core/filter.c

- BPF_PROG_TYPE_LWT_SEG6LOCAL: net/core/filter.c

- BPF_PROG_TYPE_LIRC_MODE2: drivers/media/rc/bpf-lirc.c

- BPF_PROG_TYPE_SK_REUSEPORT: net/core/filter.c

- BPF_PROG_TYPE_FLOW_DISSECTOR: net/core/filter.c

- BPF_PROG_TYPE_CGROUP_SYSCTL: kernel/bpf/cgroup.c

- BPF_PROG_TYPE_RAW_TRACEPOINT_WRITABLE: kernel/tracing/bpf_trace.c

- BPF_PROG_TYPE_CGROUP_SOCKOPT: kernel/bpf/cgroup.c

- BPF_PROG_TYPE_TRACING: kernel/tracing/bpf_trace.c

- BPF_PROG_TYPE_LSM: kernel/bpf/bpf_lsm.c

- BPF_PROG_TYPE_SK_LOOKUP: net/core/filter.c

- BPF_PROG_TYPE_SYSCALL: kernel/bpf/syscall.c

Program arguments

As you may have noticed in *Code 3.1*, each BPF program has an argument attached to the program function definition. The definition of the arguments will vary between BPF program types. You can use these program arguments (sometimes called program context) like you would in any other regular function. As we go through each program type in *Chapter 7, eBPF Observability*, *Chapter 8, eBPF Networking*, and *Chapter 9, eBPF Security*, we will explain these arguments.

Loops

Until Linux kernel version 5.3, the number of instructions a BPF program was allowed to run was 4096, and loops of any kind were not permitted by the verifier. A set of patches from *Alexei Starovoitov* allows for bounded loops, limited to one million instructions (set by **BPF_COMPLEXITY_LIMIT_INSNS** in **bpf.h**). As shown in the code example, this loop runs 3 times (well under the limit) and prints the loop index each time it runs:

```
SEC("kprobe/__sys_connect")
int trace_sys_connect(struct pt_regs *ctx)
{
    for (int i = 0; i < 3; i++) {
        char fmt[] = "Running loop %d";
        bpf_trace_printk(fmt, sizeof(fmt), i);
    }
    return 0;
}
```

In kernel 5.17, there was a new **bpf_loop()** helper function added to the kernel:

long bpf_loop(u32 nr_loops, void *callback_fn, void *callback_ctx, u64 flags)

You can see how the helper is used to manage the loop in the following code example:

```
#include "vmlinux.h"
#include <bpf/bpf_helpers.h>
#include "bpf_misc.h"

u32 nr_loops;
```

```
static int empty_callback(__u32 index, void *data)
{
    return 0;
}
SEC("kprobe/__sys_connect")
int test_loops(void *ctx)
{
    for (int i = 0; i < 1000; i++) {
        bpf_loop(nr_loops, empty_callback, NULL, 0);
    }
    return 0;
}
```

This helper allows you to run loops in a simple manner with a set of protections (outside of the eBPF verifier) to ensure that the loop is not infinite or too large.

Tail calls

In kernel 4.2, a new feature was added that allows one BPF program to call another BPF program (up to a maximum number of 32 calls) known as BPF tail calls.

When a tail call is initiated from one BPF program to another, it passes the original BPF program context to the newly called program. The newly called program is responsible for returning a return code back to the initial program caller.

Only eBPF programs of the same program-type can be tail called. They also need to match in the means that they are complicated, meaning either JIT compiled or only interpreted programs can be invoked, but cannot be mixed together.

Tail calls are particularly useful for packet filtering and processing. Each BPF program can be used for performing one piece of filtering logic instead of having to make a much longer program. This makes it easier to unit-test your BPF program as well.

Sleepable programs

In kernel version 4.14, new functionality to support sleepable programs was added. This means that BPF programs can sleep and wait for a specific time or event to occur safely. This can be used to trace operations that may be blocking like large memory allocations or locking operations.

You should be careful and thoroughly test eBPF sleepable programs to ensure that they do not cause system instability or other issues.

Program return codes

As is common with most programs or functions, an eBPF program must always return an integer (a return code). The effect of these return codes varies with each program type, but they can symbolize whether or not to allow a specific packet or action. You will notice these prominently in XDP programs, but also in programs with various security applications. As we walk through each program type in *Chapter 7, eBPF Observability*, *Chapter 8, eBPF Networking*, and *Chapter 9, eBPF Security*, we will discuss the meaning of these return codes.

bpftool

In order to debug all these eBPF primitives, it is prudent to have some tooling available to debug BPF programs. A common tool that is used for debugging BPF programs in user-space is the **bpftool** CLI utility.

The **bpftool** command allows you to do the following actions:

- Loading and unloading BPF programs and maps
- Listing available BPF programs and maps
- Inspecting the properties and contents of BPF programs and maps
- Uploading new BPF programs and maps to the kernel
- Detaching BPF programs from specific kernel hooks or events
- View what BPF features are available in your system

You may find that **bpftool** is not bundled with your distribution, so you may have to compile it yourself by running the following commands:

```
$ git clone --recurse-submodules https://github.com/libbpf/
bpftool.git
$ cd bpftool/src
$ sudo make install
```

This will compile the tool and install it at **/usr/local/sbin/bpftool**.

You can quickly test if it works by running the following command:

```
$ sudo bpftool feature
```

It should display a lengthy print-out of all the kernel configuration, BPF programs, BPF maps and BPF helpers available for you to use. At this point, many of them should look familiar to you.

If you would like more information about the basic debug functions available in **bpftool**, this blog post is an excellent primer: **https://qmonnet.github.io/whirl-offload/2021/09/23/bpftool-features-thread/**.

Conclusion

As this chapter has shown, there are a large number of programming primitives in the eBPF ecosystem that provide the ability to flexibly interact with a large portion of the kernel.

In this chapter, we have introduced the primitives of eBPF programming. Firstly explain the **BPF()** system call which is now the gateway to interacting with the eBPF subsystem. Secondly, we reviewed other primitives, program types, attach types, and their helpers. We then reviewed map helpers and other helper functions. Thirdly, we looked at program arguments, loops, tail calls, and return codes. Finally, we looked at **bpftool** which is the default tool for debugging the eBPF primitives that we have discussed in this chapter.

In the next chapter, we will look at the different libraries and frameworks available to write eBPF programs with.

Join our book's Discord space

Join the book's Discord Workspace for Latest updates, Offers, Tech happenings around the world, New Release and Sessions with the Authors:

https://discord.bpbonline.com

CHAPTER 4
eBPF Programming Libraries and Frameworks

Introduction

There are many libraries and frameworks that you can write eBPF programs against. There may be several options for you depending on your skill level and interests. All of them have nearly identical capabilities. If you are considering using eBPF in production, you must take into account what programming language works best in your environment and the use of eBPF. We will talk about deployment and portability in *Chapter 6*. In this chapter, we will look at each available library and framework option.

Structure

In this chapter, we will review the following libraries, frameworks and runtimes, that can be utilized to write eBPF programs. This list of frameworks includes:

- BPF bytecode
- C and libbpf
- Perf

- BCC
- bpftrace
- ply
- gobpf
- ebpf-go
- libbpfgo
- eBPF for Windows
- libbpf-rs
- Aya
- BumbleBee
- eunomia-bpf
- bpftime

Objectives

In this chapter, we introduce a set of common eBPF libraries and frameworks that you may want to investigate and use when writing eBPF programs. The goal of this chapter is to introduce these frameworks and libraries and highlight some of their benefits and their licensing model so you can pick a library to use for writing eBPF programs.

BPF bytecode

In *Chapter 1, Classic Berkeley Packet Filter*, we looked at two examples; one was the LSF program, and the other was the Seccomp-BPF program. In these, we built BPF programs manually to perform filtering. This is comparatively tedious and error-prone, and we advise against writing these programs manually.

In eBPF, you can create **struct bpf_insn** which contains an array of eBPF instructions and then load the program using **bpf_prog_load()**.

The basic pattern to create your eBPF bytecode program is shown in the following code:

```
#include <bpf/bpf.h>

struct bpf_insn prog[] = {
    // a list of eBPF bytecode instructions
```

```
};
size_t insns_cnt = ARRAY_SIZE(prog);
LIBBPF_OPTS(bpf_prog_load_opts, opts,
    .log_buf = bpf_log_buf,
    .log_size = BPF_LOG_BUF_SIZE,
);

// using `BPF_PROG_TYPE_SOCKET_FILTER` as an example
    prog_fd = bpf_prog_load(BPF_PROG_TYPE_SOCKET_FILTER,
NULL, «GPL»,
            prog, insns_cnt, &opts);
if (prog_fd < 0) {
    printf(«failed to load prog ‹%s›\n», strerror(errno));
    return 0;
}
```

You can refer to some full examples that have been provided in the kernel source code:

- **samples/bpf/cookie_uid_helper_example.c**
- **samples/bpf/sock_example.c**
- **samples/bpf/test_cgrp2_attach.c**

While this approach is exceptionally lean, it is not particularly friendly to write the bytecode instructions. The one place where it does look practical is writing basic BPF socket filters. As we demonstrated in *Chapter 1*, you can translate a packet filter expression to bytecode.

However, given the general difficulty and readability of these bytecode programs, we will refrain from using them in any further examples in this book.

C and libbpf

C is a natural option for writing no-frills BPF programs, partly because, in most cases, you will be writing the kernel-space BPF program in C anyway. The kernel comes with libbpf built-in, which provides a set of user-space APIs that developers can use to interact with eBPF programs from user space. This includes BPF loaded that takes compiled BPF programs (object files) and loads them into the kernel. libbpf also performs verification of the program before attaching it to the appropriate kernel hook. It takes much of the boilerplate management of the BPF program, especially many of the interactions around the **bpf()** syscall.

libbpf provides the following features:

- High and low-level APIs to interact with BPF maps, attachment types, loading and unloading programs

- BPF-side APIS, including BPF helper definitions, BPF maps support, and tracing helpers, which allows developers to simplify BPF code writing.

- Support for BPF **Compile Once, Run Everywhere (CO-RE)** allowing programs to be easily portable (more on this in *Chapter 6*)

If you see **#include   <bpf/libbpf.h>** in a user-space application, you know that it uses **libbpf**. Anything that is prefixed with **bpf/** is utilizing **libbpf**.

Check out the **https://github.com/libbpf/libbpf-bootstrap** repository with simple examples of using **libbpf** to build various BPF applications. You can find the full library documentation at **https://libbpf.readthedocs.io/en/latest/api.html**.

libbpf is packaged in the kernel. It is dual-licensed under BSD 2-clause license and GNU LGPL v2.1 license. You can choose between one of them, if you use this work.

Perf

Perf is a Linux profiling **command line interface (CLI)** utility that is popular (especially before perf has some support for eBPF). It allows you to run BPF programs via the perf utility.

eBPF support was added to perf in 2015[1] (in Linux 4.4) to perf in more recent years. It allows you to perform richer tracing, combining the utility of perf with the rich tracing abilities of eBPF. By using perf with eBPF, developers can perform dynamic tracing, analyze network performance, perform user-level profiling, and analyze disk performance, providing a comprehensive view of system performance.

Brendan Gregg's perf blog post (**https://www.brendangregg.com/perf.html#eBPF**) has more information on how to use this.

---

1. https://lwn.net/Articles/650608/

BCC

The **BPF Compiler Collection** (**BCC**) project (**https://github.com/iovisor/bcc/**) is an open source collection of libraries and tools available in Python, C++ and Lua. The project was started by *Brendan Gregg* in 2014 and has become one of the most recognizable pieces of software in the eBPF ecosystem. It is so because the library contains plenty of examples of writing, tracing, and networking programs and is regularly updated to support new eBPF features. For the majority of this book, we will utilize BCC as our framework of choice.

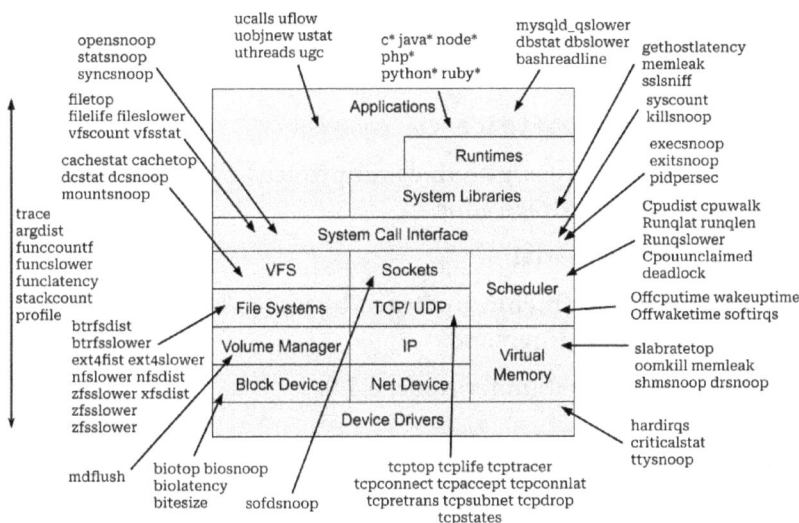

Figure 4.1: BCC tracing tools

BCC removes the need for the user to perform any compilation and removes a lot of the C language boilerplate usually required by providing a highly abstracted Python interface with a set of helpers that remove the complexity of writing eBPF programs, making it very easy to get started with. All you need to do is install the Linux kernel headers alongside BCC.

BCC is licensed under Apache-2.0.

bpftrace

The `bpftrace` (`https://bpftrace.org/`) project allows users to construct high-level eBPF one-line dynamic tracing commands. It does have a limited control of code and output. It uses the **Low**

Level Virtual Machine (LLVM) backend (more on this in *Chapter 5*) to compile strings to BPF bytecode and uses the aforementioned BCC project to interact with Linux's eBPF interface.

bpftrace provides a simple language (similar to awk) for writing eBPF tracing programs (and was inspired by awk, DTrace and SystemTap). It also includes a growing library of built-in tracing functions that can be used to probe various system and application-level events, such as system calls, kernel functions, disk I/O, and network activity.

One of the best features of **bpftrace** is the ability to write one-liner programs to perform complex tasks for example:

```
bpftrace -e 'tracepoint:raw_syscalls:sys_enter { @[comm] =
count(); }'
```

To learn more about **bpftrace**, you can visit:

- **Manual:** **https://github.com/bpftrace/bpftrace/blob/master/ man/adoc/bpftrace.adoc**

- **One-liner tutorial:**

  https://github.com/bpftrace/bpftrace/blob/master/docs/ tutorial_one_liners.md

  BCC is licensed under Apache-2.0.

ply

ply (**https://github.com/iovisor/ply**) is a dynamic tracer for Linux which is built upon eBPF. It has been designed with embedded systems in mind. It is written in C and all that ply needs to run is libc and a modern Linux kernel with eBPF support, meaning, it does not depend on LLVM for its program generation. It has a C-like syntax for writing scripts, is heavily inspired by awk and dtrace and is exceptionally similar to **bpftrace**. Refer to the following *Code 4.3*:

```
ply 'kprobe:sys_* { @syscalls[caller] = count(); }'
```

Documentation and language references are available at **wkz.github. io/ply.**

ply is licensed under GPL-2.0.

gobpf

gobpf (**https://github.com/iovisor/gobpf**) is a library that allows you to load and use eBPF programs from golang. It provides Golang bindings to the BCC framework and Go-based interface to eBPF that is relatively similar to BCC Python. While gobpf is a simple move from BCC Python to Go, it has not been updated recently and there is better options.

gobpf is licensed under Apache-2.0.

ebpf-go

ebpf-go (**https://github.com/cilium/ebpf/**) is an up-to-date pure Go library to run and interact with BPF programs. The library contains a set of utilities for compiling, loading and debugging eBPF programs. It requires a kernel version > 4.9.

The library is somewhat unique in that it allows you to write eBPF assembly instructions directly within your Go code as well as compiling and embedding eBPF programs written in C within Go code. As well as compiling the C code, it auto generates Go code for loading and manipulating the eBPF program.

ebpf-go is licensed under MIT.

libbpfgo

libbpfgo (**https://github.com/aquasecurity/libbpfgo**) is a Go-based library for working with eBPF by *Aqua Security* (a company that is at the forefront of container security). The standard use of libbpfgo is as follows:

- You write and compile your BPF program yourself into an object file.
- In your Go program, you create a new Module from opening the compiled BPF program.
- Create a new program BPFProg by loading the Module.
- Attach the program to the appropriate system attachment point
- Currently, your program is running in the kernel.
- Create maps if required and interact with the data.

You can find the documentation for the project at: **https://pkg.go.dev/ github.com/aquasecurity/tracee/libbpfgo**

libbpfgo is licensed under Apache-2.0.

eBPF for Windows

In 2021, *Microsoft* announced that it would support eBPF on Windows and open source it (**https://github.com/microsoft/ebpf-for-windows**). This means that developers will be able to use eBPF to write programs that can be executed in the Windows kernel, which can provide fast and efficient packet filtering and tracing capabilities. eBPF for Windows project exposes libbpf APIs to provide source code compatibility for applications that interact with eBPF on both Windows and Linux.

Microsoft provides the reference architecture, as shown in *Figure 4.2*, for building, verification and execution of eBPF programs in the Windows ecosystem:

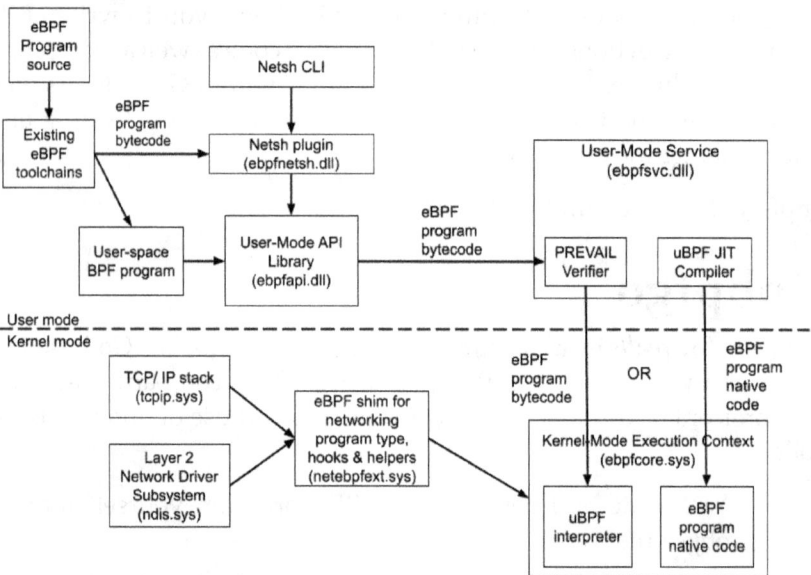

Figure 4.2: eBPF for Windows architecture

Documentation for eBPF for Windows can be found on its GitHub page.

eBPF for Windows is licensed under MIT.

libbpf-rs

libbpf-rs (**https://github.com/libbpf/libbpf-rs**) is a no-frills Rust programming language wrapper around the libbpf library. It provides a very similar user-space interface to libbpfgo. libbpf-rs handles the compilation of your kernel-space program and then allows you to easily interact with your program from user-space, including injecting global variables into the eBPF program. libbpf-rs supports CO-RE.

You can find documentation for the project at: **https://docs.rs/libbpf-rs/latest/libbpf_rs/**

libbpf-rs is available under the Apache-2.0.

Aya

Aya eBPF library is a Rust-based library for working with eBPF programs on Linux. Aya does not have dependencies on libbpf or BCC and is completely Rust native. It utilizes the libc to interact with the kernel and supports CO-RE.

You can find more about aya at: **https://aya-rs.dev/**

Aya is licensed under the MIT License.

BumbleBee

BumbleBee is an open-source tool by *Solo.io* that brings a Docker like experience to eBPF application development. It provides a CLI interface that allows you to build, package, and deploy eBPF programs as OCI-compliant images, which can be run in containerized environments. By automating boilerplate code creation and utilizing libbpf, BumbleBee simplifies the initial development process for eBPF projects.

You can find more information about BumbleBee at: **https://github.com/solo-io/bumblebee/**

BumbleBee is available under the Apache-2.0.

eunomia-bpf

eunomia-bpf is a library / runtime that aims to make distributing eBPF programs easier. It allows you to easily build and run CO-RE eBPF applications as well as package eBPF applications as **WebAssembly (Wasm)** programs. This approach makes eBPF accessible for users unfamiliar with kernel development, as it abstracts lower-level complexities and integrates with WebAssembly for enhanced portability. Finally, it allows you to create, utilize and run pre-compiled OCI image eBPF programs.

You can find more information about eunomia-bpf at: **https://github.com/eunomia-bpf/eunomia-bpf**

eunomia-bpf is licensed under the MIT License.

bpftime

bpftime is a user-space runtime framework that provides the primitives to compile and run eBPF programs in user-space. It allows you to write generic programs that can either be executed as kernel-space eBPF programs or bypassing some kernel constructs to run eBPF programs on machines where kernel-eBPF is unavailable.

You can find more information about bpftime at: **https://github.com/eunomia-bpf/bpftime**

bpftime is licensed under the MIT License.

Conclusion

As you have seen in this chapter, there are many options when it comes to picking an eBPF library. While much of the available functionality in these libraries is the same, the licensing of the project and the level of abstraction will play an important part in your choice of framework.

In the next chapter, we will now write some introductory eBPF programs in C, Python, Go, and Rust. In *Chapter 10, eBPF Open Source Projects and the Future of eBPF,* we will further discuss some of the popular projects built on some of these libraries.

Join our book's Discord space

Join the book's Discord Workspace for Latest updates, Offers, Tech happenings around the world, New Release and Sessions with the Authors:

https://discord.bpbonline.com

CHAPTER 5
Writing Your First eBPF Program

Introduction

So far, we have mostly covered extended eBPF in a theoretical sense. This chapter will demonstrate how we can write our first eBPF programs. In this book, we will mostly utilize the BCC framework to write example programs. It provides a good mix of functionality/ control with complexity. However, in this chapter, we will cover a number of programming frameworks so no matter your preferred language, you know how to get started.

In this chapter, we are first going to write an example **BPF_PROG_TYPE_ KPROBE** (more details about this program type can be found in *Chapter 7, eBPF Observability*), that looks for the clone syscall and prints **Hello World!**, and then write a second program that uses a map to capture the number of times a particular syscall was invoked by each process.

Structure

In this chapter, we will cover the following topics:

- Setting up your development environment

- Programming in Python with BCC
- Writing eBPF programs with C and libbpf
- Writing eBPF Go programs with ebpf-go
- Writing eBPF Rust programs with libbpf-rs
- BPF headers
- Best practices

Objectives

In this chapter, we aim to introduce the basics of writing eBPF programs using four different programming libraries. By the end of this chapter, you should be able to write, compile, and run an eBPF program on your machine.

Setting up your development environment

It is recommended that you use a recent distribution release and run a 5.x or 6.x kernel. As noted earlier in *Chapter 3, eBPF Programming Concepts*, some features will not be available if you are on an older kernel (you can see features by kernel version in Appendix A). It is worth noting that some eBPF features get backported into older kernel versions. However, you should always check (and test) for compatibility. We will discuss the portability of eBPF programs further in *Chapter 6, eBPF Portability and Deploying*.

Firstly, your kernel should be configured in the following manner to support various eBPF functions. You can check your (BPF) kernel settings by running the following command to see your kernel's BPF-related configuration:

```
$ grep BPF /boot/config-$(uname -r)
CONFIG_BPF=y
CONFIG_BPF_SYSCALL=y

# [optional, for tc filters]
CONFIG_NET_CLS_BPF=y

# [optional, for tc actions]
CONFIG_NET_ACT_BPF=y
```

```
CONFIG_BPF_JIT=y

# [for Linux kernel versions 4.1 through 4.6]
CONFIG_HAVE_BPF_JIT=y

# [for Linux kernel versions 4.7 and later]
CONFIG_HAVE_EBPF_JIT=y

# [optional, for kprobes]
CONFIG_BPF_EVENTS=y
```

Or by running: **bpftool feature | grep CONFIG_**

There are a few optional kernel flags needed for running BCC networking examples on a vanilla kernel:

```
$ grep BPF /boot/config-$(uname -r)
CONFIG_NET_SCH_SFQ=m
CONFIG_NET_ACT_POLICE=m
CONFIG_NET_ACT_GACT=m
CONFIG_DUMMY=m
CONFIG_VXLAN=m
```

Now that our system is ready for use, let us start programming. You can find the full examples in **/ch05** of the book's code repository.

Programming in Python with BCC

Python is a great place to start with eBPF due to the simplicity of writing and running programs. The BCC library (**https://github.com/iovisor/bcc/**) has become well-known for providing tools that provide basic observability functions. The figures below show traditional Linux observability tools and their eBPF counterparts. There is a full detailed installation guide (**https://github.com/iovisor/bcc/blob/master/INSTALL.md**) that covers multiple OS architectures as well as building from source. We will summarize it here.

Installing prerequisites

Before we use BCC, we need to install the BCC library package. Given below are the instructions to install BCC for Python system:

- **Red Hat/Centos BCC tools installation**:
    ```
    $ sudo yum install bcc bcc-doc bcc-tools
    ```

- **Ubuntu BCC tools installation:**

```
$ sudo apt install bpfcc-tools linux-headers-$(uname
-r) bpfcc-tools
```

  Note: For Debian and Ubuntu users.

- **Amazon Linux (AMI):**

```
$ sudo amazon-linux-extras enable BCC
$ sudo yum install kernel-devel-$(uname -r)
$ sudo yum install bcc
```

You can find more detailed BCC installation instructions in the installation guide (**http://github.com/iovisor/bcc/blob/master/INSTALL.md**).

Unfortunately, there is no recently released PyPi package of BCC that is only installed into your virtual environment. Hence for any references of BCC in this Chapter, we will avoid any references to Python virtual environments.

Programming with BCC

The BCC project has become well-known for providing tools that provide basic observability functions. The figures below show traditional Linux observability tools and their eBPF BCC counterparts.

These example tools are a great way to get a feel for writing reasonably simple eBPF programs. You can find more about these tools at the BCC project page: **https://github.com/iovisor/bcc**

Displaying data

The BCC libraries provide some helper functions for displaying data, which is useful when writing observability programs:

- **bpf_trace_printk()**: A simple kernel facility for **printf()** to the common **trace_pipe** (**/sys/kernel/debug/tracing/trace_pipe**). This is adequate for some quick proof-of-concepts, but has some limitations: 3 args max, 1 use of **%s** only, and **trace_pipe** is globally shared, so concurrent programs will have clashing output.

- **trace_print()**: Prints the data from the **trace_pipe** into the user space program.

- **trace_fields()**: This method reads one line from the globally shared **trace_pipe** and returns it as fields.

- **print_linear_hist()**: Prints a table as a linear histogram in ASCII. This is intended to visualize small integer ranges, e.g, 0 to 100.

- **print_log2_hist()**: Prints a table as a log2 histogram in ASCII. The table must be stored as log2, which can be done using the BPF function **bpf_log2l()**.

Writing your first program with BCC

The BCC reference guide (**https://github.com/iovisor/bcc/blob/master/docs/reference_guide.md**) provides a mostly complete reference into writing easy to intermediate level BPF programs.

The first program we are going to write will print a message from kernel-space to user-space when the **sys_clone** syscall is invoked. You can find this example program in the GitHub repository **/ch05/BCC**:

```
from bcc import BPF

BPF(text='int kprobe__sys_clone(void *ctx) { bpf_trace_
printk("Hello, World!\\n"); return 0; }').trace_print()
```

from bcc import BPF imports the BPF class, which essentially acts as the interface to the BPF machine in the kernel.

At the second line, we instantiate a BPF program. The **text** argument references the kernel-space program.

If we look at the construction of this program:

- **int kprobe__sys_clone(void *ctx)**: This indicates that we are intercepting the **sys_clone** function via kprobes. Every time the **sys_clone** syscall is invoked, the code within this function will be executed.

- **bpf_trace_printk("Hello, World!\ \n")**: This is an eBPF helper function which acts in a similar manner to **printf()** and writes the text into the common **trace_pipe** (**/sys/kernel/debug/tracing/trace_pipe**). This tracing pipe is limited to three arguments and is also shared globally, so if you are running multiple programs writing to the pipe, there will be clashing outputs.

- **return 0**: Necessary formality for a Kprobe program.

- **trace_print()**: Reads from the **trace_pipe**, 1024 characters at a time, and prints the message back to the user-space program.

If you run this program, and in another terminal, run commands like **ls, who**, and **last**, you will see **Hello World** printed in the terminal for each command that you run.

This program can also be written in the following manner:

```
from bcc import BPF

# define BPF program
kernel_prog = """
int kprobe__sys_clone(void *ctx) {
    bpf_trace_printk("Hello, World!\\n");
    return 0;
}
"""
prog = BPF(text=kernel_prog)
while 1:
    prog.trace_print()
```

You can then run your program by running:

```
$ sudo python3 hello_world.py
```

Every time the syscall **sys_clone** is called, your program will print **Hello World!**.

Note: To run most eBPF programs, you must run it with root privileges. There are some exceptions to this, we will discuss that in Chapter 6, eBPF Portability and Deploying.

Using maps and helpers with BCC

Now that we have written our first eBPF program using the bare basics of eBPF programming, we are going to write a new program that counts the number of times that the **clone()** syscall is used by each process, store it in a map and then print that map when the program is interrupted by *control+C/command+C* (a **KeyboardInterrupt**).

In this second example, instead of including the C program in the same file as our Python program, we are going to load and read from a separate C file **example2.c**:

```
#include <linux/ptrace.h>

BPF_HASH(clone_count, u32);

int count_sys_clone(struct pt_regs *ctx)
{
        u32 pid = bpf_get_current_pid_tgid() >> 32;
        u64* count = clone_count.lookup(&pid);
        if (count) {
            (*count)++;
        } else {
            u64 val = 1;
            clone_count.update(&pid, &val);
        }
        return 0;
}
```

In this program, we define a map (**BPF_MAP_TYPE_HASH**) using the macro **BPF_HASH**. The map is called **clone_count**, and the map key is of type unsigned 32-bit integer (**u32**).

We then define a custom function called **count_sys_clone** in which we retrieve the **process ID (PID)** of the Linux task that triggered the BPF program using the BPF helper **bpf_get_current_pid_tgid()** and then we check if we a count object for in our map using the **lookup()** function, and if it does not exist, we create it, if it does, we increment the current count for the process using the **update()** function. We then return **0** (more on that in *Chapter 7, eBPF Observability*).

We will also create a Python user-space program in **example2.py**:

```
from bcc import BPF

bpf = BPF(src_file = "example2.c")

# Attach BPF program to kprobe
bpf.attach_kprobe(event="sys_clone",    fn_name="count_sys_
clone")

# Retrieve the BPF map
clone_count_map = bpf.get_table("clone_count")

# Sleep to allow tracing
while True:
```

```
try:
    bpf.perf_buffer_poll()
except KeyboardInterrupt:
    break

for pid, count in clone_count_map.items():
    print(f"Process ID: {int(pid)}, Count: {count.value}")
```

In the Python program, we load a source file (**src_file**) **example2.c,** and then manually attach a Kprobe. We attach it to the **sys_clone** kernel function, which triggers the **count_sys_clone** eBPF kernel-space function. This step would have been skipped if we had named the eBPF function **int kprobe__sys_clone(void *ctx)**.

Then, we open the BPF hash map defined in user-space by calling **bpf. get_table("clone_count")**.

A while loop runs waiting for a **KeyboardInterrupt** (*control+C/ command+C*) and then once we hit interrupt, we print out the values of the map which contains the process ID and the count of **clone** calls.

You can find the full example at **ch05/BCC/example2**.

Writing eBPF programs with C and libbpf

Writing eBPF programs in C is a very common practice, given the direct bindings to libbpf. libbpf has a large number of user-space APIs. A full list can be found here: **https://libbpf.readthedocs.io/en/latest/ api.html**

Installing prerequisites

Before we get started, we need to have **clang**, **libelf** and **zlib** packages available.

Redhat/Centos BCC tools installation:

```
$ sudo dnf install clang elfutils-libelf elfutils-libelf-
devel zlib-devel
```

Ubuntu BCC tools installation:

```
$ sudo apt install clang libelf1 libelf-dev zlib1g-dev
```

Amazon Linux (AMI):

```
$ sudo yum install clang elfutils-libelf elfutils-libelf-
devel zlib-devel
```

Writing your first program with libbpf

With libbpf, we write a separate C file for our BPF program, which then gets compiled into an object file and then loaded by your user-space program. You can see an example of a BPF program **kprobe. bpf.c** below:

```c
#include "vmlinux.h"
#include <bpf/bpf_helpers.h>
#include <bpf/bpf_tracing.h>
#include <bpf/bpf_core_read.h>

char LICENSE[] SEC("license") = "GPL";

SEC("kprobe/sys_clone")
int BPF_KPROBE(kprobe_clone, int __syscall_nr, const char
* filename, const char *const * argv, const char *const *
envp)
{
    pid_t pid;
    pid = bpf_get_current_pid_tgid() >> 32;
    bpf_printk("Starting kernel function 'sys_clone' (pid
= %d)\n", pid);
    return 0;
}
```

Now, we need a user-space program to load and attach the BPF program. We do this for a few sections. You can find the full example in **ch05/libbpf/example1/**. First, we need to perform our standard imports, set up our printing function, and create a signal intercept function that stops the program looping:

```c
#include <stdio.h>
#include <unistd.h>
#include <signal.h>
#include <string.h>
#include <errno.h>
#include <sys/resource.h>
#include <bpf/libbpf.h>
```

```
#include "kprobe.skel.h"

static int libbpf_print_fn(enum libbpf_print_level level,
const char *format, va_list args)
{
    return vfprintf(stderr, format, args);
}

static volatile sig_atomic_t stop;

static void sig_int(int signo)
{
    stop = 1;
}
```

We will now write our main function below:

```
int main(int argc, char **argv)
{
    struct kprobe_bpf *skel;
    int err;

    /* Set up libbpf errors and debug info callback */
    libbpf_set_print(libbpf_print_fn);

    /* Open load and verify BPF application */
    skel = kprobe_bpf__open_and_load();
    if (!skel) {
        fprintf(stderr, "Failed to open BPF skeleton\n");
        return 1;
    }

    /* Attach tracepoint handler */
    err = kprobe_bpf__attach(skel);
    if (err) {
        fprintf(stderr, "Failed to attach BPF skeleton\n");
        goto cleanup;
    }

    if (signal(SIGINT, sig_int) == SIG_ERR) {
        fprintf(stderr, "can't set signal handler: %s\n",
strerror(errno));
        goto cleanup;
    }
```

```
    printf("Successfully started! Please run `sudo cat /
sys/kernel/debug/tracing/trace_pipe` "
            "to see output of the BPF programs.\n");

    while (!stop) {
        fprintf(stderr, ".");
        sleep(1);
    }
cleanup:
    kprobe_bpf__destroy(skel);
    return -err;
}
```

In our main function, we first set up our printing function, then load and verify the compiled BPF program. Once the program is loaded, it then needs to be attached to the kernel. At this point of time, our program is running. We can interrupt the program by pressing *control+C* or *command+C*. Unlike BCC, libbpf does not have a native user-space printing function so you will have to **cat** the **trace_pipe**.

Note: You cannot use tail; you must use cat.

Copy the Makefile from **ch05/libbpf-c/example1** and then run make in your terminal.

Using maps and helpers with libbpf

We will now write a second example using maps and helpers.

```
#include "vmlinux.h"
#include <bpf/bpf_helpers.h>
#include <bpf/bpf_tracing.h>

// Defines a hash map called 'clone_count' which can contain
8192 entries, has a key type of pid_t and a value type of
u64.
struct {
    __uint(type, BPF_MAP_TYPE_HASH);
    __uint(max_entries, 8192);
    __type(key, pid_t);
    __type(value, u64);
} clone_count SEC(".maps");
```

```
SEC("kprobe/sys_clone")
int bpf_prog1(struct pt_regs *ctx)
{
    // Get the current user-space program PID
    u32 pid = bpf_get_current_pid_tgid() >> 32;

    // Check if an entry is in the hash map 'clone_count'
for the given PID
    u64* count = bpf_map_lookup_elem(&clone_count, &pid);

    if (count) {
        (*count)++;
    } else {
        u64 val = 1;
        // Create the map entry for the user-space PID
        bpf_map_update_elem(&clone_count, &pid, &val, BPF_
ANY);
    }
    return 0;
}

char _license[] SEC("license") = "GPL";
```

In **example2.bpf.c**, the structure of our program is reasonably similar, however, a number of the macros that BCC provided in the previous section are now replaced with standard BPF functions:

- The **clone_count.lookup()** is replaced with **bpf_map_lookup_elem(&clone_count, &pid)**

- The **clone_count.update()** is replaced with **bpf_map_update_elem(&clone_count, &pid, &val, BPF_ANY)**

On the user-space side, we write a new function to iterate through the map and print the process ID and the count of **open_at()** syscalls:

```
void print_clone_count(struct bpf_map *clone_count_map) {
    if (!clone_count_map) {
        fprintf(stderr, "Error: clone_count_map is
NULL\n");
        return;
    }
```

```
    fprintf(stdout, "Process count:\n");

    int key, next_key, value;

    key = 0;
    while (bpf_map__get_next_key(clone_count_map, &key,
&next_key, sizeof(next_key)) == 0) {
        if(bpf_map__lookup_elem(clone_count_map, &next_
key, sizeof(next_key), &value, sizeof(__u64), 0) == 0) {
            printf("PID: %u, `clone` syscall count: %u\n",
next_key, value);
        } else {
            fprintf(stderr, "Failed to lookup element for
key: %u\n", next_key);
        }
        key = next_key;
    }
}
```

Then, in the mail function, we follow the same pattern to load and attach the BPF kernel-space program, but then we wait for the **INT** signal (a keyboard interrupt), which then triggers our **print_clone_count()** function:

```
int main(int argc, char **argv) {
    struct example2_bpf *skel;
    int err;
    struct bpf_map *clone_count_map;

    /* Set up libbpf errors and debug info callback */
    libbpf_set_print(libbpf_print_fn);

    /* Open, load, and verify BPF application */
    skel = example2_bpf__open_and_load();
    if (!skel) {
        fprintf(stderr, "Failed to open and load BPF
skeleton\n");
        return 1;
    }

    /* Attach tracepoint handler */
    err = example2_bpf__attach(skel); // Use the skeleton's
```

```
attach function
    if (err) {
        fprintf(stderr, "Failed to attach BPF skeleton:
%s\n", strerror(-err)); // More informative error message
        goto cleanup;
    }

    clone_count_map = bpf_object__find_map_by_name(skel-
>obj, "clone_count"); // Use skel->obj
    if (!clone_count_map) {
        fprintf(stderr, "Failed to find clone_count map\n");
        goto cleanup;
    }

    if (signal(SIGINT, sig_int) == SIG_ERR) {
        fprintf(stderr, "can't set signal handler: %s\n",
strerror(errno));
        goto cleanup;
    }

    while (!stop) {
        fprintf(stderr, ".");
        sleep(1);
    }
    // Print open count
    print_clone_count(clone_count_map);

cleanup:
    example2_bpf__detach(skel); // Detach before closing
    example2_bpf__destroy(skel); // Use destroy instead of
individual frees and closes.
    return err;
}
```

You can again use the **Makefile** from **ch05/libbpf-c/example2** and then run **make** in your terminal to build and run the program.

If you want a full introduction into libbpf, the libbpf-bootstrap (**https://github.com/libbpf/libbpf-bootstrap/**) repository provides a detailed guide that includes multiple program types.

Writing eBPF Go programs with ebpf-go

As mentioned in *Chapter 4, eBPF Programming Libraries and Frameworks,* ebpf-go allows you to compile separate eBPF C programs straight into your Go program. You do not need to install any additional system packages to start using ebpf-go.

Install prerequisites

If you program regularly in Go, you can move on to the next section. However, before we get started with ebpf-go, we should ensure that we have all of the prerequisites installed:

1. We need to remove any existing Go binaries that may have been installed onto your system by running **rm -rf /usr/ local/go**.

2. Now you need to **https://go.dev/dl/** and download the latest Go release that matches your system. Since it is most likely that you will be using a Linux machine, we are going to find the latest Linux Archive release for x86_64. At the time of writing, this happens to be **https://go.dev/dl/go1.20.4.linux-386.tar.gz**. Download the latest Linux release and save it in your **/usr/ local** directory.

3. Then we will untar the downloaded archive: **tar -C /usr/ local -xzf go1.20.4.linux-368.tar.gz**.

4. Now, let us add **/usr/local/go/bin** to the **PATH** environment variable. We can do this by adding the following line to your **$HOME/.profile or /etc/profile** (for a system-wide installation): **export PATH=$PATH:/usr/local/go/bin**.

5. Now run source **$HOME/.profile**, and your system should be ready to run Go.

6. Run **go version** and you should see something like this:
   ```
   $ go version
   go version go1.20.4 linux/amd64
   ```

Writing your first program

In this example, we are again going to write a simple Kprobe program that prints **Hello, world** every time the **sys_clone** kernel function is called.

First, we start with the eBPF C program, **kprobe.c**:

```
//go:build ignore

#include <linux/bpf.h>
#include <bpf/bpf_helpers.h>

char __license[] SEC("license") = "Dual MIT/GPL";

SEC("kprobe/sys_clone")
int kprobe_clone() {
        const char fmt[] = "Hello, world!\n";
        bpf_trace_printk(fmt, sizeof(fmt));
        return 0;
}
```

We then write the user-space program in Go, **main.go**:

```
package main

import (
    "fmt"
    "log"
    "os"
    "os/signal"
    "syscall"

    "github.com/cilium/ebpf/link"
    "github.com/cilium/ebpf/rlimit"
)
//go:generate go run github.com/cilium/ebpf/cmd/bpf2go -cc
clang bpf kprobe.bpf.c -- -I../headers

func main() {
    // Name of the kernel function to trace.
    fn := "sys_clone"

      // Allow the current process to lock memory for eBPF
```

```
resources.
    if err := rlimit.RemoveMemlock(); err != nil {
        log.Fatal(err)
    }

    // Load the pre-compiled program into the kernel.
    objs := bpfObjects{}
    if err := loadBpfObjects(&objs, nil); err != nil {
        log.Fatalf("loading objects: %v", err)
    }
    defer objs.Close()

        // Open a Kprobe at the entry point of the kernel
function and attach the
    // pre-compiled program.
    kp, err := link.Kprobe(fn, objs.KprobeClone, nil)
    if err != nil {
        log.Fatalf("opening kprobe: %s", err)
    }
    defer kp.Close()

    log.Println("Kprobe attached. Waiting for events (Ctrl+C
to exit)...")

    // Handle Ctrl+C signal for graceful shutdown
    sigchan := make(chan os.Signal, 1)
    signal.Notify(sigchan, syscall.SIGINT, syscall.SIGTERM)

    // Keep running until Ctrl+C is pressed
    <-sigchan

        fmt.Println("\nExiting...") // Print a message before
exiting
}
```

We can then compile and run our eBPF program:

```
$ go mod init github.com/michaelkkehoe/ch05/ebpf-go/
example1
$ go tidy
$ go generate
$ go build
$ sudo ./example1
```

In another terminal, run cat to see the output of the program:

```
sudo cat /sys/kernel/debug/tracing/trace_pipe
```

This will build a new program called **kprobe**. You can now run **sudo go run.** and you will see **Hello, world** be printed every time the clone syscall is called.

Unlike BCC, ebpf-go does not provide any helper functions for printing or displaying data, however, there are a large number of helper functions provided by the library to interact with programs and maps.

Using maps and helpers with ebpf-go

For our second ebpf-go example, we again write a BPF program in using code that is again nearly identical to our **krpobe.bpf.c** libbpf example earlier. You will note that for the kernel programs in ebpf-go, you do not need to provide the program arguments.

```
//go:build ignore

#include "common.h"

char __license[] SEC("license") = "Dual MIT/GPL";

struct bpf_map_def SEC("maps") clone_count = {
    .type        = BPF_MAP_TYPE_HASHMAP,
    .key_size    = sizeof(u32),
    .value_size  = sizeof(u64),
    .max_entries = 1,
};

SEC("kprobe/sys_clone")
int kprobe_sys_clone() {
    u32 key     = 0;
    u64 initval = 1, *valp;

    valp = bpf_map_lookup_elem(&kprobe_map, &key);
    if (!valp) {
            bpf_map_update_elem(&clone_count, &key, &initval,
BPF_ANY);
        return 0;
    }
    __sync_fetch_and_add(valp, 1);

    return 0;
}
```

In the user-space ebpf-go program, we open and load our skeleton, and then open the Kprobe. Then we wait for the **KeyboardInterrupt** and iterate over the map and print its contents:

```go
func main() {

        // Name of the kernel function to trace.
        fn := "sys_clone"

        // Allow the current process to lock memory for eBPF
resources.
        if err := rlimit.RemoveMemlock(); err != nil {
                log.Fatal(err)
        }

        // Load the pre-compiled program into the kernel.
        objs := bpfObjects{}
        if err := loadBpfObjects(&objs, nil); err != nil {
                log.Fatalf("loading objects: %v", err)
        }
        defer objs.Close()

        // Open a Kprobe at the entry point of the kernel
function and attach the
        // pre-compiled program.
        kp, err := link.Kprobe(fn, objs.KprobeClone, nil)
        if err != nil {
                log.Fatalf("opening kprobe: %s", err)
        }

        clone_counter, err := objs.clone_count
        if err != nil {
                log.Fatalf("Failed to get BPF map: %v", err)
        }

        // Wait for a KeyboardInterrupt signal to stop the
program
        sig := make(chan os.Signal, 1)
        signal.Notify(sig, syscall.SIGINT, syscall.SIGTERM)
        <-sig

        fmt.Println("Tracing clone() calls. Press Ctrl+C to
stop.")

        ticker := time.NewTicker(5 * time.Second)
```

```
        defer ticker.Stop()

    iter := clone_counter.Iterate()
    for iter.Next(&key, &val) {
        fmt.Println("Process ID: %u, Count: %llu\n", key,
value);
    }
}
```

You can find detailed documentation at: **https://pkg.go.dev/github. com/cilium/ebpf**.

Writing eBPF Rust programs with libbpf-rs

Now, we will take a look at writing eBPF programs with Rust and libbpf-rs.

Installing prerequisites

If you are new to Rust, you can easily get started by running this installer:

```
$ curl https://sh.rustup.rs | sh
```

This will get the basics installed onto your system.

Writing your first libbpf-rs program

We are now going to create a new Rust project by running:

```
$ cargo new libbpf-rs-example1
```

This will generate a new directory called **libbpf-rs-example1** with the following files:

```
$ dir
|- Cargo.toml
|- src
  |- main.rs
```

- **Cargo.toml** is the manifest file for Rust. It is where you keep metadata for your project, as well as dependencies.

- **src/main.rs** is where we will write our application code.

We are going to add **libbpf-rs** as a dependency to our new project by running it inside the new **libbpf-rs-example1** directory that was just created:

```
$ cargo add libbpf-rs
```

We will also need to create a **build.rs** file in our root project directory so that Rust is able to compile our kernel-space eBPF program:

```rust
use libbpf_cargo::SkeletonBuilder;
use std::env;
use std::path::PathBuf;

const SRC: &str = "src/bpf/kprobe.bpf.c";

fn main() {
    let mut out =
        PathBuf::from(env::var_os("OUT_DIR").expect("OUT_
DIR must be set in build script"));
    out.push("kprobe.skel.rs");
    SkeletonBuilder::new()
        .source(SRC)
        .build_and_generate(&out)
        .unwrap();
    println!("cargo:rerun-if-changed={SRC}");
}
```

We also add a new basic BPF program in **src/bpf/kprobe.bpf.c**:

```c
#include "vmlinux.h"
#include <bpf/bpf_helpers.h>
#include <bpf/bpf_tracing.h>

char __license[] SEC("license") = "Dual MIT/GPL";

SEC("kprobe/sys_clone")
int BPF_KPROBE(sys_clone, struct pt_regs *regs) {
    const char fmt[] = "Hello, world!\n";
    bpf_trace_printk(fmt, sizeof(fmt));
    return 0;
}
```

Then, finally, we complete our already created **main.rs** file:

```rust
use std::thread::sleep;
use std::time::Duration;

use anyhow::Result;

mod kprobe{
```

```
    include!(concat!(env!("OUT_DIR"), "/kprobe.skel.rs"));
}

use kprobe::*;

fn main() -> Result<()> {
    let mut skel_builder = kprobeskelBuilder::default();
        let mut open_skel = skel_builder.open()?;
    let mut skel = open_skel.load()?;
    skel.attach()?;

    // Block until SIGINT
    loop {
            sleep(Duration::new(1, 0));
    }
}
```

Now we can build and run our new program:

```
$ cargo build
$ sudo target/debug/libbpf-rs-example1
```

In another terminal, run **cat** to see the output of the program:

```
$ sudo cat /sys/kernel/debug/tracing/trace_pipe
```

You still begin to see the application printing **Hello World!**.

Using maps and helpers with libbpf-rs

For the second libbpf-rs program, we can utilize the same **build.rs** and **cargo.toml** files as well as the kernel-space eBPF program we have used for the libbpf-c and epf-go examples with maps.

For the user-space program, we again follow the same pattern to load the skeleton and attach it to the kernel. We then open the map and wait for the **SIGINT** signal and then iterate over the map to print the contents:

```
use std::thread::sleep;
use std::time::Duration;

use anyhow::Result;
use byteorder::{ByteOrder, LittleEndian}; // Import
byteorder crate
use libbpf_rs::{Map, MapFlags};
```

```
mod kprobe{
    include!(concat!(env!("OUT_DIR"), "/kprobe.skel.rs"));
}

use kprobe::*;

fn main() -> Result<()> {
    let mut skel_builder = kprobeskelBuilder::default();
    let mut open_skel = skel_builder.open()?;
    let mut skel = open_skel.load()?;
    skel.attach()?;

    sleep(Duration::new(30, 0));

    // Process BPF map entries after exiting the loop
    // Access the map (using the map name from your BPF
program)
    let maps = skel.maps(); // Store the maps object
    let map = maps.clone_count(); // Now we have a
reference to the specific map
    let mut key_iter = map.keys();
    while let Some(key) = key_iter.next() {
        // Ensure the key is 4 bytes (a u32), and convert
it to u32
        // Lookup the value (count) for this pid
        let pid: u32 = LittleEndian::read_u32(&key);
        // let pid: u32 = key.as_slice().try_into().
expect("Key is not 4 bytes");
        match map.lookup(&key, MapFlags::empty()) {
            Ok(Some(value)) => {
                let count: u64 = LittleEndian::read_
u64(&value);
                println!("PID: {}, Count: {}", pid, count);
            }
            Ok(None) => {
                println!("PID not found: {}", pid);
            }
            Err(e) => {
                eprintln!("Error looking up PID {}: {}",
pid, e);
```

```
        }
      }
    }
    Ok((())
}
```

BPF headers

As you may have noticed in the kernel-space eBPF programs, there is usually a set of **includes** macros to import BPF header files. These headers are included to access specific BPF related functions. You can find the source for these in **tools/lib/bpf/** of the Linux kernel. The list below is a synopsis of what each header file is for (these files may be removed or renamed with new releases):

- **bpf/bpf_core_read.h**: This is a set of helper functions to read values from kernel structures. You can find an excellent guide to these functions on *Andrii Nakryiko's* blog (**https://nakryiko.com/posts/bpf-core-reference-guide/**). We will talk more about this in *Chapter 6, eBPF Programming Libraries and Frameworks*.

- **bpf/bpf_endian.h**: Helper functions for swapping byte order.

- **bpf/bpf_helpers.h**: A wrapper file to that includes BPF helpers.

- **bpf/bpf_tracing.h**: The **bpf_tracing.h** header file provides definitions, data structures, and functions that are used for writing BPF programs specifically for tracing and profiling purposes.

- **bpf/bpf.h**: It is the main BPF header. It contains the complete list of all helper functions, as well as many other BPF definitions, including most of the flags, structs or constants used by the helpers.

- **bpf/btf.h**: A set of helpers to support BTF. We will discuss this further in *Chapter 6, eBPF Portability and Deploying*.

- **bpf/hashmap.h**: Generic non-thread safe hash map implementation.

- **bpf/libbpf.h**: Headers that contain all of the **libbpf.h** helpers.

- **bpf/nlattr.h**: BPF Netlink interface.

- **bpf/usdt.bpf.h**: The **bpf/usdt.bpf.h** header file provides definitions, data structures, and functions for working with

USDT probes in BPF programs. It includes helper functions and macros that simplify the process of attaching BPF programs to USDT probes and extracting information from the probes at runtime.

Best practices

Before the chapter ends, here are a few things to keep in mind when writing eBPF programs:

1. You want your kernel-space programs to be as efficient as possible.

2. With respect to the previous point, each kernel-space eBPF program can only be 4096 instructions long.

3. You essentially have unlimited space for BPF Maps; however, ensure that you do not use all of your container/machine memory on them. Also, keep in mind that the more items you have in your maps, the longer it may take to perform operations on that data.

4. As mentioned precedingly, using **bpf_trace_printk()** is acceptable for simple demos, but not ideal for large-scale setups where one needs to print multiple arguments or compete with other programs writing to the shared **trace_pipe**. If you need to send information from user-space, you pass it using a map or a ring-buffer.

5. The programs run as root and can modify the behavior of a machine in many ways. While eBPF provides safety mechanisms to the user and the kernel, you can still cause disruption to the system.

Conclusion

This chapter has provided an introduction into how you can write your first eBPF program using a set of different framework options. In the next chapter, we will cover how to make your eBPF programs portable and how to deploy them across a fleet of compute.

Join our book's Discord space

Join the book's Discord Workspace for Latest updates, Offers, Tech happenings around the world, New Release and Sessions with the Authors:

https://discord.bpbonline.com

CHAPTER 6
eBPF Portability and Deploying

Introduction

Now that we have introduced how to write basic programs, we should also talk about how to write, compile, and deploy at scale! This chapter will introduce you to the BTF, CO-RE, and, later, will cover some of the challenges of deploying BPF programs across a fleet of machines.

Structure

In this chapter, we will cover the following topics:

- BPF Type Format
- CO-RE
- BPFtool
- BPF deployment approaches
- BPF deployment frameworks
- Notes for fleet-wide deployment

Objectives

In this chapter, you will learn how to take the basic BPF programs written and get them production-ready to deploy across multiple platforms. We will also learn about some of the theories behind BPF portability and the philosophy of CO-RE, as well as some testing and deployment strategies.

BPF Type Format

So far in this book, we have covered the primary case of writing code that runs on the same machine it is compiled on. Once you start using eBPF beyond your desktop, your BPF programs must be portable. Having portable BPF programs means building and verifying a BPF program on one machine and executing the same program on multiple Linux kernel versions without recompilation.

Most programming languages have debuggers that can provide visibility into the program, such as **GNU Debugger (GDB)**, which can be used for C, C++, or Golang. These debuggers rely on the DWARF debugging format. While **debugging with attributed record formats (DWARF)** has worked well for these user-space applications, it is not particularly friendly for BPF due to the number of kernel structs that BPF programs may potentially access.

The kernel documentation succinctly describes BTF:

BTF (BPF Type Format) is the metadata format that encodes the debug info related to the BPF program/map. The name BTF was used initially to describe data types. The BTF was later extended to include function info for defined subroutines and line info for source/line information.

The debug info maps pretty print, function signature, etc. The function signature enables a better BPF program/function kernel symbol. The line info helps generate source annotated translated byte code, jited code, and verifier log.

Reference: https://www.kernel.org/doc/html/latest/bpf/btf.html

It is a file format that encodes the type of information of a BPF program and provides better introspection and visibility into the program. If you have written C or C++ before, you may have utilized GDB to perform debugging operations. Until the introduction of BTF, inspecting a BPF program was impossible.

It was introduced into the kernel in version 4.18 and has continued to evolve in later kernel versions. BTF is far more space-efficient than DWARF and allows you to describe all types of information in a BPF program. It can be enabled by having your kernel configuration set to `CONFIG_DEBUG_INFO_BTF=y`.

You can find much more information about the inner workings of BTF on these pages:

- **https://docs.kernel.org/bpf/btf.html**
- **https://www.airplane.dev/blog/btf-bpf-type-format**

CO-RE

BPF CO-RE allows you to write your code and compile it once and have the ability to run it on a variety of Linux systems (e.g., systems running different kernel versions).

As we will explore the remainder of this book, eBPF programs will regularly need to access fields within specific kernel data structures. Before CO-RE, you would need to compile a copy of your BPF program against each kernel version header so the compiler could correctly locate these fields, as they occasionally change between kernel versions due to the lack of the same data structures. For example, if you were to compile an eBPF program against a 5.2 kernel and try to run the same binary on a 5.6 kernel, there is no guarantee that the program would execute.

In the primary examples we have looked at using BCC, when the program is invoked, Clang/LLVM using the kernel-headers package we installed and compiles the program on the fly. There are several disadvantages to this method, as you will read about in the *eBPF deployment approaches* section of this chapter.

CO-RE simplifies the portability issue by using BTF as well as functionality in the Clang compiler to represent data structure layouts on the machine the program was compiled and provides a method to locate those same fields on a target host running the same compiled program (as long as the data structure exists on the target hosts kernel).

There are four components to BPF CO-RE:

- **BTF**: It represents the relocation information required to run the program (The kernel must be running with option **CONFIG_ DEBUG_INFO_BTF=y**).

- **Clang**: This was extended to emit the BTF relocation information in the compiled **Executable and Linkable Format (ELF)** binary. The compiler captures the structs, field names, and field types (as well as map access information) that your BPF program wants to access and stores that so it can be correctly mapped to the same struct on a target machine even if the struct layout is different. This is called field offset relocation.

- **BPF loader**: This is typically provided by libbpf, but the loader knows how to process the BPF ELF binary and set up the program and maps. The loader will process the BPF binary's BTF type and relocation information and map that to the BTF information on the local machine. It will update the program if needed (but will not recompile it) and then execute it.

- **libbpf helper functions**: These functions are a wrapper to safely read data from the kernel and verify the existence of objects.

Reading data in a BPF CO-RE application

libbpf contains a set of helpers designed for you to safely access data from the kernel in a CO-RE-compatible manner. Similarly, the library has a set of functions that allow you to safely verify that an object exists before you try to access it. Here are some common non-CO-RE and CO-RE equivalents:

Task	Non-CO-RE function	CO-RE function
Read data	`bpf_probe_read()`	`bpf_core_read()`
Read a string	`bpf_probe_read_str()`	`bpf_core_read_str()`
Reading data (easier to use)	`bpf_probe_read()`	`BPF_CORE_READ()`
Read directly into a variable	`bpf_probe_read_kernel()`	`BPF_CORE_READ_INTO()`
Read a string directly into a variable	`BPF_PROBE_READ_STR_INTO`	`BPF_CORE_READ_STR_INTO()`

Table 6.1: Libbpf Non-CO-RE and CO-RE reading functions.

Handling kernel changes and feature mismatch

You may also need to account for verifying if a field, a struct, an enum, or a BPF feature exists within your BPF program. libbpf provides some helpers to help you safely check if something exists before you use it. Here is a non-exhaustive list of these functions:

Task	Function
Verify if a field within a struct exists	`bpf_core_field_exists()`
Verify type existence (mostly used for verifying if structs exist)	`bpf_core_type_exists()`
Verify if an enum value exists	`bpf_core_enum_value_exists()`
Get the version of the Linux kernel that is running	`extern int LINUX_KERNEL_VERSION __kconfig;`

Table 6.2: *libbpf data verification helpers*

It is recommended to read the following blog posts by *Andrii Nakryiko* (an eBPF kernel developer) for further detailed information about CO-RE:

- **https://nakryiko.com/posts/bpf-portability-and-co-re/**
- **https://nakryiko.com/posts/bpf-core-reference-guide/**
- **https://nakryiko.com/posts/bcc-to-libbpf-howto-guide/**
- **https://nakryiko.com/posts/libbpf-bootstrap/**

This blog post (**https://www.sartura.hr/blog/simple-ebpf-core-application**) by *Juraj Vijtiuk* is also useful for understanding how to write a basic sample eBPF CO-RE application. There is also limited information about these helper functions in the libbpf official documentation.

BPFtool

As briefly discussed in *Chapter 3, eBPF Programming Concepts*, bpftool is a command line utility that allows users to interact with the BPF subsystem in the Linux kernel. It has become the standard means to interact with the BPF Linux subsystem.

In this section, we are going to introduce some basic operations that you can perform using the **bpftool** utility (**https://man.archlinux. org/man/bpftool.8**). The basic commands are:

- **bpftool**: The basic top-level command

- **bpftool version**: Prints the version of the utility

- **bpftool batch file**: Runs commands in batch mode from a file.

- **bpftool map**: Inspection and simple manipulation of eBPF maps

- **bpftool prog**: Inspection and simple manipulation of eBPF progs

- **bpftool link**: Inspection and simple manipulation of eBPF links

- **bpftool cgroup**: Inspection and simple manipulation of cgroup eBPF programs

- **bpftool perf**: Inspection of perf related bpf prog attachments

- **bpftool net**: Inspection of networking related bpf prog attachments

- **bpftool feature**: Inspection of eBPF-related parameters for Linux kernel or net device

- **bpftool btf**: Inspection and dumping of BTF data

- **bpftool gen**: BPF code-generation

- **bpftool struct-ops**: Register/unregister/introspect BPF `struct_ops`

- **bpftool iter**: Create BPF iterators

We will now run through some essential **bpftool** functions.

Loading and managing BPF programs

bpftool allows users to load BPF programs into the kernel. This includes both eBPF programs and classic BPF programs.

The basic command syntax to do that is:

```
$ bpftool prod load <object file path> /sys/fs/bpf/<program name>
```

Where **object file path** is the path to a BPF compiled object file and **program name** is a unique BPF program name that you set. It does not have to correlate to a file or function name, for example:

```
$ bpftool prog load my_program.o /sys/fs/bpf/my_program
```

There is no manner in **bpftool** to unload a BPF program at the time or writing, however, you can unload your program from the kernel by deleting the pinned pseudo file like so:

```
$ rm /sys/fs/bpf/<program name>
$ rm /sys/fs/bpf/my_program
```

If you are loading or unloading BPF programs that are attached to cgroups, you can use the **bpftool cgroup** command. More information and examples can be found on the bpftool-cgroup(8) man page.

Querying BPF programs

bpftool allows you to query the different types of BPF objects, which include programs, maps, and links, giving you a view of the eBPF ecosystem on the host. You can list out all running programs on a host by running **bpftool prog list** or **bpftool prog show**. This provides an output in the following output:

```
32: cgroup_device  tag 03b4eaae2f14641a  gpl
    loaded_at 2023-12-08T14:19:41-0800  uid 1000
    xlated 296B  jited 163B  memlock 4096B  map_ids 1
33: cgroup_device  tag 03b4eaae2f14641a  gpl
    loaded_at 2023-12-08T14:19:44-0800  uid 1000
    xlated 296B  jited 163B  memlock 4096B  map_ids 2
535: cgroup_device  tag ee0e253c78993a24  gpl
    loaded_at 2023-12-11T16:29:17-0800  uid 0
    xlated 416B  jited 256B  memlock 4096B
    pids systemd(1)
```

Let us briefly understand the fields for the first program in this output:

- The program ID is **32**.
- The program type is **cgroup_device**.
- There is no name for the program.
- The tag (which is an alternate identifier) is **03b4eaae2f14641a**.
- The program uses a GNU GPL-compatible license.

- The program was loaded into the kernel at **2023-12-08T14:19:41-0800**.
- The user ID that loaded the program is **1000** (You can look in **/etc/passwd** to match this to a username).
- There are **296** Bytes of eBPF bytecode in the program.
- The program has **163** Bytes of machine code.
- The program has reserved **4096** Bytes (4k) of memory that will not be paged out.
- The program may reference/use eBPF map ID **1**.

You can query BPF programs using the BPF program ID, the name of the program, the tag, or by the virtual filesystem location known as the **pinned path**.

```
$ bpftool prog show id 540
$ bpftool prog show name my_program
$ bpftool prog show tag d35b94b4c0c10efb
$ bpftool prog show pinned /sys/fs/bpf/my_program
```

Inspecting BPF maps

bpftool provides the ability to examine BPF maps, which are data structures used for communication between the user space and the BPF programs.

```
$ bpftool map show
$ bpftool map show id 7
```

Which gives you an output similar to this:

```
1: hash   flags 0x0
    key 9B   value 1B   max_entries 500   memlock 8192B
2: hash   flags 0x0
    key 9B   value 1B   max_entries 500   memlock 8192B
3: hash   flags 0x0
    key 9B   value 1B   max_entries 500   memlock 8192B
4: hash   flags 0x0
    key 9B   value 1B   max_entries 500   memlock 8192B
```

You can also dump the contents of the map:

```
$ bpftool map dump id 1
$ bpftool map dump id 1 -pretty
```

Which gives an output similar to this:

```
$ bpftool map dump id 1 --pretty
[{
        "key": ["0x63","0x8a","0x00","0x00","0x00",
"0xff","0xff","0xff","0xff"
        ],
        "value": ["0x01"
        ]
        },{
        "key": ["0x63","0xe2","0x00","0x00","0x00",
"0x00","0x00","0x00","0x00"
        ],
        "value": ["0x01"
        ]
        },{
        "key": ["0x63","0x01","0x00","0x00","0x00",
"0x05","0x00","0x00","0x00"
        ],
        "value": ["0x01"
        ]
        }
}]
```

Verifying BPF programs

The utility can be used to perform a basic verification of BPF programs before they are loaded into the kernel. This helps catch potential issues with the program before it is loaded into the kernel:

```
$ bpftool prog test my_program.o
```

Dumping BPF program disassembly

Users can disassemble BPF programs to view the generated instructions. This can be useful for debugging and performance optimization. However, it does require a good amount of assembly and low-level programming languages:

```
$ bpftool prog disasm id 1
```

Attaching BPF programs

As we will discuss later in the book, some eBPF program types are attached to specific kernel hooks rather than events like kprobesor uprobes. Unlike those tracing programs, there needs to be a way to indicate what kind of kernel hook you are attaching to. This is done in the **BPF()** syscall, but is also exposed to the user in the **bpftool net attach** command. For example, an **xdp** program (with ID 1) is attached to the **eth0** network interface:

```
$ bpftool net attach xdp id 1 dev eth0
```

You can also **detach** the program with:

```
$ bpftool net detach xdp dev eth0
```

bpf net attach works for the following program types:

- **BPF_PROG_TYPE_XDP**
- **BPF_PROG_TYPE_SCHED_CLS**
- **BPF_PROG_TYPE_SCHED_ACT**
- **BPF_PROG_TYPE_FLOW_DISSECTOR**
- **BPF_PROG_TYPE_NETFILTER**

For programs that are attached to cgroups, for example:

- **BPF_PROG_TYPE_CGROUP_SKB**
- **BPF_PROG_TYPE_CGROUP_SOCK**
- **BPF_PROG_TYPE_SOCK_OPS**
- **BPF_PROG_TYPE_CGROUP_SOCK_ADDR**

You can use the **bpftool cgroup** command to manipulate cgroup attachments.

BPF deployment approaches

The rest of this chapter will cover the in-depth of how to deploy BPF programs beyond a single device to fleets of machines.

The naive method

The naive method of deploying BPF applications is to utilize BCC to write and run applications. As a reminder, BCC utilizes the Clang/ LLVM toolchain to recompile the BPF application every time it is executed using the locally installed kernel headers. Running ad hoc, one off BPF applications using BCC is not necessarily a bad solution as you would have to compile the application at least once.

However, if you are deploying a BPF application to a fleet of machines using BCC, you will likely come across issues with this approach, namely:

- You need to deploy BCC (which includes Clang and LLVM toolchains) as well as kernel headers on to every machine that you want to run eBPF applications on. This means that every target machine needs to be able to distribute these packages reliably and it will also take up storage space on the target machine.

- Every execution of the eBPF application on each host will result in a recompilation of the program and this can utilize a significant amount of system resources.

- Testing your programs does become more complex as you need to test your program against every kernel header's variation.

For a proof of concept or a place where you have limited time/effort resources, this solution is not unreasonable, however, if you are deploying in a production environment at any kind of scale, there will be overheads.

A better way

As you may have guessed, a better way to build and deploy BPF applications that will be used in production environments is to utilize CO-RE supported libraries. This allows you to write applications that you can confidently run on numerous kernel/OS configurations without worrying about compatibility.

In *Chapter 4, eBPF Programming Libraries and Frameworks*, we briefly introduced libbpf and libbpf-bootstrap which is the simplest way to write user-space and CO-RE compatible kernel-space eBPF programs. The libbpf-bootstrap project provides a large set of examples on how to write CO-RE eBPF programs and user-space loaders. This blog post also walks through creating a BPF program loader using the primitives in libbpf.

BPF deployment frameworks

While it is more than possible to write your own BPF program and loader, there are some options to use specialist tooling for running BPF programs.

systemd

systemd has become ubiquitous in Linux in recent times. systemd has added a number of new features that utilize eBPF programs to provide the functionality. These are:

- RestrictFileSystems
- RestrictNetworkInterfaces
- IPIngressFilterPath
- IPEgressFilterPath
- DeviceAllow
- BPFProgram

RestrictFileSystems

RestrictFileSystems allows you to create an allow list or deny list of files system types the systemd service can access. For example, you can allow the service to only access **tmpfs** file systems by setting **RestrictFileSystems=tmpfs**. You can also deny which filesystems are available by specifying which filesystem types are not allowed. For example, **RestrictFileSystems=~tracefs**. This feature adds an extra layer of security preventing processes from accessing security sensitive file systems like **debugfs** or **tracefs** even if they are running as root.

RestrictNetworkInterfaces

Similar to RestrictFileSystems, systemd allows you to limit the network interfaces that a systemd service can have access to. For example, if you specify **RestrictNetworkInterfaces lo0**, the processes within the systemd service can only utilize the loopback interface on the host. You can also create a deny list instead that blocks access to certain interfaces, for example, **RestrictNetworkInterfaces=~wg0** which blocks access to the **wg0** interface. This feature requires kernel >= 5.7.

IPIngressFilterPath and IPEgressFilterPath

Takes an absolute path to a pinned BPF program in the BPF virtual filesystem **/sys/fs/bpf/</filename>**. This allows you to reference a pinned **BPF_PROG_TYPE_CGROUP_SKB** program to act as an IP traffic filter. Multiple BPF programs can be specified and apply to all IP packets sent/received under the **INET/INET6** sockets created by processes of the unit, in addition to any other filters of the system. You will have to load the BPF programs yourself. A great end-to-end tutorial on how to use this feature is available at: **https://kailueke.gitlab.io/systemd-custom-bpf-firewall/**.

DeviceAllow

This allows you to specify a device access control list (reading/writing/creating) using the **BPF_PROG_TYPE_CGROUP_DEVICE** BPF program type. This feature was added in systemd version 208. You can find more information on how to use it at: **https://www.freedesktop.org/software/systemd/man/latest/systemd.resource-control.html#DeviceAllow=**.

BPFProgram

BPFProgram allows you to attach your own BPF program to a cgroup of a unit. Only certain types of BPF programs are allowed. The BPF program type is equivalent to the BPF attach type used in bpftool(8) It may be one of **egress, ingress, sock_create, sock_ops, device, bind4, bind6, connect4, connect6, post_bind4, post_bind6, sendmsg4, sendmsg6, sysctl, recvmsg4, recvmsg6, getsockopt, or setsockopt**. The specification of BPF program consists of a pair of BPF program type and program path in the file system, with **:** as the separator: **type:program-path**.

Some basic examples of this behavior include:

```
BPFProgram=egress:/sys/fs/bpf/egress-hook
BPFProgram=bind6:/sys/fs/bpf/sock-addr-hook
```

This functionality was added in Systemd version 249.

Deploying your application with bpftool and systemd

You can use systemd to manage the start/stop of your eBPF program:

```
[Unit]
Description=cgroup socket drop filter
```

```
[Service]
Type=oneshot
RemainAfterExit=yes
ExecStart=/path/to/bpftool prog load /path/to/cgroup-sock-
drop.o /sys/fs/bpf/cgroup-sock-drop-filter type cgroup/skb
ExecStop=rm /sys/fs/bpf/cgroup-sock-drop-filter
LimitMEMLOCK=infinity
```

This very simply uses **bpftool** to load a BPF program object file and pins it to **/sys/fs/bpf/cgroup-sock-drop-filter**. It will also unload the BPF program when the service is stopped.

bpfman

bpfman — **https://bpfman.io** (formally known as bpfd) is a platform that allows you to manage the deployment and monitoring of BPF programs on a single host or in a Kubernetes cluster.

bpfman is a software stack that aims to make it easy to load, unload, modify, and monitor eBPF programs whether on a single host or in a Kubernetes cluster. bpfman includes the following CO-RE components:

- **bpfman**: A system daemon that supports loading, unloading, modifying, and monitoring of eBPF programs on a single host exposed over a gRPC API.

- **Kubernetes Custom Resource Definitions**: bpfman provides a set of **Custom Resource Definitions** (**CRDs**) that allow you to express the BPF programs configuration in a Kubernetes Cluster.

- **bpfman-agent**: An agent that manages the state of bpfman managed programs and ensures they are in the desired state.

- **bpfman-operator**: An operator that manages the installation and lifecycle of bpfman-agent.

greggd

greggd (**https://github.com/olcf/greggd**) is a runtime that allows you to daemonize eBPF programs and emit their outputs to a socket for consumption (for tracing program types). It allows you to take raw BPF program source code and then attach the BPF program to multiple different kprobesusing YAML configuration instead of manually modifying the program. It also allows you to specify a schema of your program's output to then be piped into a socket.

Notes for fleet-wide deployment

Before you complete this chapter, you should note some real-world challenges with deploying BPF applications in production systems.

Feature compatibility

While BTF and CO-RE allow you to run programs across kernel versions, they do still need to be compatible. As we will lay out in the upcoming chapters, a lot of BPF program types (and associated features) were introduced in a particular kernel version. Depending on what OS you are running, this feature may be available on an earlier or later version than what appears in the BPF features by Linux kernel version page (**https://github.com/iovisor/bcc/blob/master/docs/kernel-versions.md**).

You can also run **bpftool feature** on a collection of OS/kernel versions to confirm that the BPF feature you need is available.

You can also ask the system at runtime to validate if the program is running on a kernel version you believe you need by evaluating **extern int LINUX_KERNEL_VERSION __kconfig;**

Privileges and compatibility

Given eBPF's close proximity to the kernel, applications generally have to be run with Linux system privileges (known as capabilities).

If you look at the Linux sysctl **kernel.unprivileged_bpf_disabled**, it should be set to the value **2** which represents **only privileged users enabled**. While it is not recommended, in a development environment, it could set it to **0** for convenience so you do not have to be a privileged user to test programs. This is highly discouraged in any other use-case.

Most of the time, when you use **sudo** on a Linux system, you will be granted a large set of capabilities.

CAP_BPF

eBPF applications generally require the Linux capability **CAP_SYS_**

ADMIN to execute. This is a high-level privilege that gives you near-full administrative privileges on a host. You should create a separate user and not run your eBPF programs as **root**. A new capability was created known as **CAP_BPF** was added to the kernel in version 5.8, which provides some extra security to your system.

CAP_BPF allows the split of BPF operations that are allowed under **CAP_SYS_ADMIN** into a combination of **CAP_BPF, CAP_PERFMON, CAP_NET_ADMIN** and keep some of them under **CAP_SYS_ADMIN**.

CAP_BPF helps solve three problems:

- Providing isolation between user space processes that drop **CAP_SYS_ADMIN** and switch to **CAP_BPF**.

- Enhances security for BPF networking programs as **CAP_BPF + CAP_NET_ADMIN**.

- Enables fuzzers to test all of the verifier logic as a privileged user which allows a more extensive set of verifier logic to be run.

CAP_BPF has the ability to perform the following operations:

- Create all types of BPF maps.
- Execute advanced BPF verifier features.
- Load BTF data.
- Retrieve translated and JITed code of BPF programs.

You can find more information about **CAP_BPF** on Milan's blog post: **https://mdaverde.com/posts/cap-bpf/**.

BPF program types and capatabilities

In **kernel/bpf/syscall.c**, within the **static int bpf_prog_** `load()` function is the kernel logic to determine what capabilities are required to run BPF programs:

eBPF program type	Capability required
BPF_PROG_TYPE_SOCKET_FILTER BPF_PROG_TYPE_CGROUP_SKB	None
BPF_PROG_TYPE_SCHED_CLS BPF_PROG_TYPE_SCHED_ACT BPF_PROG_TYPE_XDP BPF_PROG_TYPE_LWT_IN: BPF_PROG_TYPE_LWT_OUT: BPF_PROG_TYPE_LWT_XMIT: BPF_PROG_TYPE_LWT_SEG6LOCAL: BPF_PROG_TYPE_SK_SKB: BPF_PROG_TYPE_SK_MSG: BPF_PROG_TYPE_FLOW_DISSECTOR: BPF_PROG_TYPE_CGROUP_DEVICE: BPF_PROG_TYPE_CGROUP_SOCK: BPF_PROG_TYPE_CGROUP_SOCK_ADDR BPF_PROG_TYPE_CGROUP_SOCKOPT BPF_PROG_TYPE_CGROUP_SYSCTL: BPF_PROG_TYPE_SOCK_OPS BPF_PROG_TYPE_EXT BPF_PROG_TYPE_NETFILTER	CAP_NET_ADMIN CAP_SYS_ADMIN
BPF_PROG_TYPE_CGROUP_SKB	CAP_NET_ADMIN (to attach)
BPF_PROG_TYPE_SK_REUSEPORT SOCKET_FILTER	CAP_BPF
BPF_PROG_TYPE_KPROBE: BPF_PROG_TYPE_TRACEPOINT: BPF_PROG_TYPE_PERF_EVENT: BPF_PROG_TYPE_RAW_TRACEPOINT: BPF_PROG_TYPE_RAW_TRACEPOINT_WRITABLE BPF_PROG_TYPE_TRACING BPF_PROG_TYPE_LSM BPF_PROG_TYPE_STRUCT_OPS BPF_PROG_TYPE_EXT	CAP_PERFORM CAP_SYS_ADMIN

Table 6.3: BPF program and required system capability matrix

Unit testing

Like any other production code, eBPF programs should also be unit-tested. Given that BPF programs are running within kernel-space, it is even more important to be writing unit-tests. If you look closely enough in the kernel source code, you will notice a large number of unit test files.

Unit testing in eBPF is not that different from any other application. In this case, we are going to have the following components:

- BPF program that we want to test.
- Unit test.
- A Makefile.
- The BPF skeleton loader.
- A Bash script to setup the environment and tear it down (optional).

You are able to run tests that validate the value of variables defined in your BPF program or the return value of your BPF program.

The following is a simple demonstration of unit-testing a simple XDP-based firewall (**xdp_firewall.bpc.c**):

```
#include <stddef.h>
#include <linux/bpf.h>
#include <linux/in.h>
#include <linux/if_ether.h>
#include <linux/ip.h>
#include <bpf/bpf_helpers.h>
#include <bpf/bpf_endian.h>

SEC("xdp")
int drop_non_rfc1918(struct xdp_md *ctx) {
    void *data = (void *)(long)ctx->data;
    void *data_end = (void *)(long)ctx->data_end;

    struct ethhdr *eth = data;

    if (data + sizeof(*eth) > data_end) {
        return XDP_ABORTED;
    }
```

```
    if (bpf_ntohs(eth->h_proto) != ETH_P_IP) {
        return XDP_PASS;
    }

    struct iphdr *iph = data + sizeof(*eth);

    if (data + sizeof(*eth) + sizeof(*iph) > data_end) {
        return XDP_ABORTED;
    }

    __u32 src_ip = bpf_ntohl(iph->saddr);
    if ((src_ip & 0xFF000000) != 0x0A000000 &&
        (src_ip & 0xFFF00000) != 0xAC100000 &&
        (src_ip & 0xFFFF0000) != 0xC0A80000) {
        return XDP_DROP;
    }
    return XDP_PASS;
}

char _license[] SEC("license") = "GPL";
```

We have a standard **Makefile**:

```
TARGET = xdp_firewall
ARCH = $(shell uname -m | sed 's/x86_64/x86/' | sed 's/
aarch64/arm64/')

BPF_OBJ = ${TARGET:=.bpf.o}
USER_C = ${TARGET:=.c}
USER_SKEL = ${TARGET:=.skel.h}

all: $(TARGET) $(BPF_OBJ)
.PHONY: all

$(TARGET): vmlinux.h $(USER_C) $(USER_SKEL)
    gcc -Wall -o $(TARGET) $(USER_C) -L../../../libbpf/src
-l:libbpf.a -lelf -lz

%.bpf.o: %.bpf.c vmlinux.h
    clang \
        -target bpf \
        -D __TARGET_ARCH_$(ARCH) \
        -Wall \
```

```
        -O2 -g -o $@ -c $<
    llvm-strip -g $@

$(USER_SKEL): $(BPF_OBJ)
    bpftool gen skeleton $< > $@

vmlinux.h:
    bpftool btf dump file /sys/kernel/btf/vmlinux format c
> vmlinux.h

clean:
    - rm $(BPF_OBJ)
    - rm $(TARGET)
```

Let us take a look at the test runner **xdp_firewall.c**:

```
#include <stdio.h>
#include <string.h>
#include <stdlib.h>
#include <unistd.h>
#include <linux/if_ether.h>
#include <linux/ip.h>
#include <bpf/bpf.h>
#include <bpf/bpf_endian.h>
#include <arpa/inet.h>
#include "xdp_firewall.skel.h"

#define TEST_PACKET_SIZE 1500
#define ETH_P_IP 0x0800

struct ethhdr *build_ethernet_header(void *packet, unsigned
char *src_mac, unsigned char *dst_mac) {
    struct ethhdr *eth = (struct ethhdr *)packet;
    memcpy(eth->h_dest, dst_mac, ETH_ALEN);
    memcpy(eth->h_source, src_mac, ETH_ALEN);
    eth->h_proto = bpf_htons(ETH_P_IP);
    return eth;
}

struct iphdr *build_ip_header(void *packet, uint32_t src_
ip, uint32_t dst_ip) {
    struct iphdr *ip = (struct iphdr *)(packet +
sizeof(struct ethhdr));
```

```
    ip->version = 4;
    ip->ihl = 5;
    ip->tot_len = bpf_htons(sizeof(struct iphdr));
    ip->id = bpf_htons(54321);
    ip->ttl = 64;
    ip->protocol = IPPROTO_TCP;
    ip->saddr = bpf_htonl(src_ip);
    ip->daddr = bpf_htonl(dst_ip);
    return ip;
}

static inline __u32 ip_from_string(const char *ip_str) {
    __u32 ip = 0;
    int ret = inet_pton(AF_INET, ip_str, &ip);
    if (ret!= 1) {
        return 0;
    }
    return bpf_htonl(ip);
}

int test_xdp_program(struct xdp_firewall_bpf *skel, unsigned
char *src_mac, unsigned char *dst_mac, uint32_t src_ip) {
    unsigned char packet[TEST_PACKET_SIZE] = {0};
    build_ethernet_header(packet, src_mac, dst_mac);
    build_ip_header(packet, src_ip, 0xC0A80001);

    LIBBPF_OPTS(bpf_test_run_opts, opts,
        .data_in = packet,
        .data_size_in = sizeof(struct ethhdr) +
sizeof(struct iphdr) + 20 // Example
    );

    int ret = bpf_prog_test_run_opts(bpf_program__fd(skel-
>progs.drop_non_rfc1918), &opts);
    return opts.retval;
}

int main() {
    struct xdp_firewall_bpf *skel;
    int err;
```

```
    skel = xdp_firewall_bpf__open_and_load();
    if (!skel) {
        fprintf(stderr, "Failed to open and load BPF
skeleton\n");
        return 1;
    }

    err = xdp_firewall_bpf__attach(skel);
    if (err) {
        fprintf(stderr, "Failed to attach BPF program\n");
        return 1;
    }

    unsigned char src_mac[ETH_ALEN] = {0x00, 0x1a, 0x2b,
0x3c, 0x4d, 0x5e};
    unsigned char dst_mac[ETH_ALEN] = {0x01, 0x1a, 0x2b,
0x3c, 0x4d, 0x5f};
    __u32 src_ip;

    // Test with RFC1918 IP address 10.0.0.1
    int ret = test_xdp_program(skel, src_mac, dst_mac, ip_
from_string("10.0.0.1"));
    if (ret == XDP_PASS) {
        printf("[PASSED]: RFC1918 IP 10.0.0.1 allowed\n");
    } else {
        printf("[FAILED]: RFC1918 IP 10.0.0.1 should be
allowed, got %d\n", ret);
    }

    // Test with non-RFC1918 IP address 8.8.8.8
    ret = test_xdp_program(skel, src_mac, dst_mac, ip_
from_string("8.8.8.8"));
    if (ret == XDP_DROP) {
        printf("[PASSED]: Non-RFC1918 IP 8.8.8.8
dropped\n");
    } else {
        printf("[FAILED]: Non-RFC1918 IP 8.8.8.8 should be
dropped, got %d\n", ret);
    }

    // Test a boundary address (lowest in 172.16.0.0/12
range)
```

```
    ret = test_xdp_program(skel, src_mac, dst_mac, ip_
from_string("172.16.0.0"));
    if (ret == XDP_PASS) {
        printf("[PASSED]: RFC1918 IP 172.16.0.0
allowed\n");
    } else {
        printf("[FAILED]: RFC1918 IP 172.16.0.0 should be
allowed, got %d\n", ret);
    }

    xdp_firewall_bpf__destroy(skel);
    return 0;
}
```

We can then run **make all** and:

$ ./xdp_firewall

Which will execute our test and let us know if there are any errors.

Louis DeLosSantos wrote an exceptionally detailed blog post (**https:// who.ldelossa.is/posts/unit-testing-ebpf**) on how to write unit tests for eBPF programs. You will also find a large number of BPF tests within the kernel **tools/testing/selftests/bpf/** folder.

Staggered deploys

As with any piece of production software, you should thoroughly test your BPF programs before deploying them fleet-wide. Given that BPF programs are usually triggered by a low-level kernel event, and the performance profile of a production machine is different from a development desktop, there is an elevated risk with running eBPF programs.

Due diligence should be exercised in slowly rolling out a new version of an eBPF program to production systems. This talk (**https://www. youtube.com/watch?v=ZYBXZFKPS28**) by *Alexei Starovoitov* captures some of the misadventures of running eBPF programs at scale at Facebook.

Conclusion

As we conclude the theory portion of this book, you will have noticed that BPF contains a lot of complexity in the way it interacts with the kernel. Before embarking on utilizing eBPF for production use cases, thoroughly think about the environment your eBPF applications may be used in. This may drastically change the approach you take towards programming and deployment.

In the next chapter, we will apply all of the theories we have learned in the first six chapters by writing our own eBPF programs.

Join our book's Discord space

Join the book's Discord Workspace for Latest updates, Offers, Tech happenings around the world, New Release and Sessions with the Authors:

https://discord.bpbonline.com

CHAPTER 7
eBPF Observability

Introduction

While the first use of BPF started with packet filters, eBPF is best known for its observability functions. eBPF has been able to coalesce the functionality of a number of different introspection projects, including DTrace and FTrace. In this chapter, we will explain the benefits of eBPF based observability tooling and how to write your own programs.

Structure

In this chapter, we will cover the following topics:

- Introduction to eBPF observability
- Observability program types
- Using eBPF for tracing
- libbpf tracing macros
- Kprobe programs
- Tracepoint programs
- Raw tracepoint programs

- Raw tracepoint writable programs
- Perf event programs
- Picking the right program type

Objectives

In this chapter, we will explore the numerous ways you can utilize eBPF to understand both kernel and application behavior without sacrificing performance. You will learn the different observability BPF program types and how they can be applied to help you understand your system.

Introduction to eBPF observability

Until the creation of eBPF, the underlying BPF functionality had been used for network and security-based filtering purposes. As detailed in *Chapter 2, Extended Berkeley Packet Filter*, eBPF provides the ability to intercept and inspect numerous parts of the kernel with minimal overhead. This now allows us to write powerful observability tools. eBPF has an advantage over other tracing mechanisms because you can access almost all parts of the kernel with minimal overhead (or in some cases, none).

In this chapter, we are going to look at five types of BPF observability program types and their uses as means to provide observability into systems:

- Kernel probes (kprobes/Kretprobe)
- User probes (uprobes/Uretprobes)
- **User Statically-Defined Tracepoint (USDT)**
- Tracepoint probes
- Raw tracepoint probes (and raw tracepoint writeable)
- Perf events

> **Note:** eBPF provides extremely powerful functionality to understand what is happening on a system. While eBPF does offer a significant improvement on low-level tracing performance, please be mindful that eBPF programs will have a degree of performance impact that should be tested thoroughly before using them on production systems.

Observability program types

eBPF currently has six different observability program types. The components of the kernel that can be observed vary between each program type. The program types in this space are:

- **BPF_PROG_TYPE_KPROBE**: For observing kprobe/ uprobe/ USDT's/ syscalls.

- **BPF_PROG_TYPE_TRACEPOINT**: For observing tracepoints.

- **BPF_PROG_TYPE_PERF_EVENT**: For observing perf events.

- **BPF_PROG_TYPE_RAW_TRACEPOINT**: For observing tracepoints with (generally) better performance.

- **BPF_PROG_TYPE_RAW_TRACEPOINT_WRITABLE**: Same functionality as **BPF_PROG_TYPE_RAW_TRACEPOINT** but with a writable context.

While not strictly for observability purposes, many of the network related program types can be used for observability purposes. Similarly, a lot of observability programs can be used for the purpose of security monitoring controls (with caveats). We will discuss them more in *Chapter 9, eBPF Security.*

At the beginning of each subsection of this chapter (and *Chapters 8, eBPF Networking,* and *Chapter 9, eBPF Security*), we will provide an introductory technical reference guide on the programming context of each program type.

Using eBPF for tracing

In general terms, we have mentioned the benefit of eBPF as a technology that allows high-performance, low-overhead operations. There are three specific benefits to using eBPF for observability purposes:

- eBPF provides a unified means to trace both user-space and kernel-space and is compatible with a number of existing tracing tools (kprobes/uprobes/syscalls/tracepoints).

- Generally speaking, the overhead of BPF tracing programs is exceptionally better than existing tracing frameworks.

- eBPF is fully programmable, allowing you to filter, process, store, and return results within one program. You do not need to move data between different systems or programs to get a final observable product.

There are also some potential drawbacks that you will want to be aware of:

- **Portability**: While large strides have been made in this area over the past few years, diligence does need to be done to ensure that your code is compatible with different kernels and architectures.

- **Recent kernel**: To get the most up-to-date features of eBPF tracing, you need to run at least a version 5.5 kernel. Depending on your system or organization, this may not be possible.

- **Limited insights**: Generally speaking, eBPF may not provide as many insights or as much useful information as application-specific or language-specific debuggers.

libbpf tracing macros

Contained within libbpf's **bpf-tracing.h** header (**https://github.com/torvalds/linux/blob/master/tools/lib/bpf/bpf_tracing.h**) is a set of convenience wrapper macros that should make writing kernel-space programs slightly easier. These macros can be used for the observability programs defined in this chapter.

BPF_PROG

BPF_PROG is a convenience wrapper for generic BPF programs that accept input arguments as a single pointer to an untyped u64 array, where each u64 can actually be a typed pointer or integer of a different size. Instead of requiring users to write manual casts and work with array elements by index, the **BPF_PROG** macro allows the user to declare a list of named and typed input arguments in the same syntax as for normal C functions. All the casting is hidden and performed transparently, while user code can just assume working with function arguments of specified type and name.

The original raw context argument is preserved, as well as the **ctx** argument. This is useful when using BPF helpers that expect original context as one of the parameters (e.g., for **bpf_perf_event_output()**).

BPF_PROG2

BPF_PROG2 is an enhanced version of BPF_PROG in order to handle struct arguments. Since each **struct** argument might take one or two u64 values in the trampoline stack, argument type size is needed to place the proper number of u64 values for each argument. Therefore, **BPF_PROG2** has a different syntax from **BPF_PROG**. For example, for the following **BPF_PROG** syntax:

```
int BPF_PROG(test2, int a, int b) { ... }
```

The corresponding **BPF_PROG2** syntax is:

```
int BPF_PROG2(test2, int, a, int, b) { ... }
```

Where the type and the corresponding argument name are separated by a comma.

Use **BPF_PROG2** macro if one of the arguments might be a struct/union larger than 8 bytes:

```
int BPF_PROG2(test_struct_arg, struct bpf_testmod_struct_
arg_1, a, int, b,

int, c, int, d, struct bpf_testmod_struct_arg_2, e, int,
ret)
{
// access a, b, c, d, e, and ret directly
...
}
```

BPF_KPROBE

This serves the same purpose for kprobesas **BPF_PROG** does for BPF programs. It hides the underlying platform-specific low-level way of getting Kprobe input arguments from **struct pt_regs** and provides a familiar typed and named function arguments syntax and semantics of accessing Kprobe input parameters. The original **struct pt_regs** context is preserved as the program argument.

BPF_KRETPROBE

BPF_KRETPROBE is similar to **BPF_KPROBE**, except it only provides an optional return value (in addition to struct **pt_regs *ctx**).

BPF_KSYSCALL and BPF_KPROBE_SYSCALL

BPF_KSYSCALL and **BPF_KPROBE_SYSCALL** is a variant of **BPF_KPROBE**, which is intended for tracing syscall functions, like **sys_close**. It hides the underlying platform-specific low-level way of getting syscall input arguments from struct **pt_regs** and provides a familiar typed and named function arguments syntax and semantics of accessing syscall input parameters.

The original **struct pt_regs** context is preserved as program argument.

At the time of writing, **BPF_KSYSCALL** does not transparently handle all of the calling convention quirks for the following syscalls:

- `mmap()`
- `clone()`
- `socket-related syscalls`
- `compat syscalls`

BPF_UPROBE

This wraps **BPF_KPROBE** for uprobes and behaves the exact same way.

BPF_URETPROBE

This wraps **BPF_KRETPROBE** for Uretprobes and behaves the exact same way.

BCC macros

It is also worth noting that BCC also contains its own separate set of helper macros (**https://github.com/iovisor/bcc/blob/master/src/cc/export/helpers.h**) that provides some extra macros for many BPF map types as well as some additional BPF program types (**TRACEPOINT_PROBE, RAW_TRACEPOINT_PROBE, LSM_PROBE**).

Kprobe programs

The Kprobe program type is the original and most versatile eBPF observability program type. It allows you to trace kernel and user functions as well as syscalls. As we introduce each BPF program

type, we will present some basic properties of the program type in a
standard table format:

Program type name	BPF_PROG_TYPE_KPROBE
Kernel version introduced	4.1
BPF program context	**struct pt_regs** or the arguments of the function you are tracing if you're using the macro's
BPF attachment types	**BPF_TRACE_KPROBE_MULTI** (for Kprobe Multi only)
ELF sections	Kprobes: **kprobe/<function>[+<offset>]** **kretprobe/<function>[+<offset>]** Syscalls: **ksyscall/<syscall>** **kretsyscall/<syscall>** Uprobes: **uprobe[.s]/<path>:<function>[+<offset>]** **uretprobe[.s]/<path>:<function>[+<offset>]** USDTs: **usdt/<path>:<provider>:<name>** Kprobe Multi: **kprobe.multi/<pattern>** **kretprobe.multi/<pattern>**

Table 7.1: BPF_PROG_TYPE_KPROBE program attributes

Note: BPF_PROG_TYPE_{KPROBE, TRACEPOINT, PERF_EVENT, RAW_TRACEPOINT} are not subject to a stable API since kernel internal data structures can change from release to release and may, therefore, break existing tracing BPF programs. Tracing BPF programs correspond to a specific kernel that is to be analyzed, and not a specific kernel and all future ones.

We will now walk through each individual use of the Kprobe program
type.

Kprobe/Kretprobe

Kprobes enables you to observe the entry or exit of any kernel function
and collect information (arguments/return values) without disrupting
the performance of the host system.

Kprobe's are helpful to understand what happens within the execution of a syscall. If you look at all of the underlying kernel functions invoked when sending a **Transmission Control Protocol (TCP)** packet, you can imagine a Kprobe being useful to understand the performance of a particular kernel function or understand the arguments of return values of these functions. For example, as you can see in the following figure, if an application sends a TCP packet, manykernel functions are invoked within the kernel that can all be instrumented using kprobes.

Each system may have a different set of kprobesavailable for tracing. It is exceptionally important to know that kernel functions and their APIs are considered to be unstable, and their arguments could be changed, renamed, or deleted in a later kernel version. You can see the kprobesavailable on your machine by using this command:

```
$ sudo cat /sys/kernel/debug/tracing/available_filter_
functions
__startup_secondary_64
run_init_process
do_one_initcall
match_dev_by_uuid
name_to_dev_t
rootfs_mount
rootfs_mount
calibrate_delay
```

A basic Kprobe example is to profile how long it takes to complete opening a TCP connection.

You will want to attach a Kprobe at the beginning of a kernel function (e.g., **tcp_v4_connect**) and run a BPF program function to capture some information. You will then want to run a similar function for when the function returns (this is a Kretprobe) and perform some kind of data analysis.

The BPF program is defined with a hash table (named connection_start_times) that will store the start time of the kprobe.

```
BPF_HASH(connection_start_times, u32, u64, 1024);

int trace_start(struct pt_regs *ctx) {
    u32 pid = bpf_get_current_pid_tgid();
    u64 start_time = bpf_ktime_get_ns();

    connection_start_times.update(&pid, &start_time);
```

```
    return 0;
}

int trace_complete(struct pt_regs *ctx) {
    u32 pid = bpf_get_current_pid_tgid();
    u64 end_time = bpf_ktime_get_ns();
    u64 *start_time;

    start_time = connection_start_times.lookup(&pid);

    if (start_time) {
        u64 duration = end_time - *start_time;
        if (duration > 0) {
            bpf_trace_printk("%d\\n", duration / 1000);
        }
        connection_start_times.delete(&pid);
    }
    return 0;
}
```

There are two BPF program functions **trace_start** and **trace_completion**. The **trace_start** function gets the current time (in nanoseconds) and updates the hash table (eBPF map) with the triggering **pid_tgid** and the current time.

The **trace_completion** function attempts to locate the pointer to the request in the hash table, and then gets the current time and computes the time difference (in nanoseconds). It then writes to the global trace pipe the TCP connectiontime in microseconds. On the user-space side of the application, the following happens:

```
b = BPF(text=bpf_prog)
b.attach_kprobe(event="tcp_v4_connect", fn_name="trace_
start")
b.attach_kretprobe(event="tcp_send_ack", fn_name="trace_
complete")

# header
print("%-18s %-2s %-7s %8s" % ("TIME(s)", "Task", "PID",
"Duration(ms)"))

# format output
while 1:
    try:
```

```
        (task, pid, cpu, flags, ts, msg) = b.trace_fields()
        print(msg)
        ms = float(int(msg, 10)) / 1000
    except ValueError:
        continue
    except KeyboardInterrupt:
        exit()
    printb(b"%-18.9f %-16s %-6d %8.2f" % (ts, task, pid,
ms))
```

You can find this full example in the book's GitHub repository.

We recommend the following articles for further reading:

https://www.kernel.org/doc/Documentation/kprobes.txt

ksyscall/kretsyscall

The ksyscall allows you to attach eBPF programs to the entry or exit of a syscall. Like other kprobe programs, you are able to view the arguments provided to the syscall and the return value of the syscall. This was introduced in 2022.

BCC provides a helper function that helps you attach a program to a syscall. The **get_syscall_fnname()** function locates the precise syscall name required and then attaches the kernel-space function to the syscall.

```
b = BPF(text=prog)
event_name = b.get_syscall_fnname("clone")
b.attach_kprobe(event=event_name, fn_name="do_sys_clone")
```

Meanwhile, with libbpf, you can utilize the **BPF_KSYSCALL** macro to define your function and utilize **bpf_program__attach_ksyscall()** libbpf function to attach the program to syscall.

Note: You can also use the BPF_PROG_TYPE_TRACEPOINT to capture the execution (entry) of syscalls (we will talk about this more later in this chapter).

uprobe/uretprobe

The **BPF_PROG_TYPE_KPROBE** program type can also be used to trace uprobes/Uretprobes in a similar manner as kprobes. This allows you to examine functions that are in any user-space code (providing you know the function name). uprobes/uretprobes were introduced into the kernel in version 4.3.

BCC offers an **attach_uprobe()** and **attach_uretprobe()** functions to trace a function in a user-space program or a user-space program uses of an underlying library (e.g., the C library of functions).

So, if you want to trace **malloc** calls in programs written in C, you could attach uprobes like so:

```
b.attach_uprobe(name="c", sym="malloc", fn_name="alloc_
enter", pid=pid)
```

Similarly, if you wanted to trace a function in a particular binary, you could do this:

```
b.attach_uprobe(name="/usr/bin/bash", sym="readline", fn_
name="readline_enter")
```

In libbpf, you can utilize the **BPF_UPROBE/ BPF_URETPROBE** macros to define your function and attach using **bpf_program__attach_uprobe()**.

We recommend the following resources for further reading:

- **https://www.kernel.org/doc/Documentation/trace/uprobetracer.txt**
- **https://www.brendangregg.com/blog/2015-06-28/linux-ftrace-uprobe.html**

USDTs

USDT provides a user-space version of tracepoints (read more about tracepoints below). USDTs can be found in MySQL, NGINX, Node.js server, the Java JVM, and many other pieces of software.

BCC offers the ability to attach a USDT to a PID or a binary path, and then you can attach USDT probes in a similar manner to uprobes or kprobes.

To use a USDT, you create a USDT context by attaching it to a PID using the USDT class:

```
from bcc import BPF, USDT
u = USDT(pid=1234)
```

You can also attach to a library or executable:

```
from bcc import BPF, USDT
usdt_ctx = USDT(path='/usr/bin/mysql')
```

and then you enable probes using **enable_probe()**:

```
usdt_ctx.enable_probe(probe="operation_start", fn_
name="trace_operation_start")
```

You then load the BPF program as normal, but you add the USDT context:

```
bpf = BPF(text=bpf_text, usdt_contexts=[usdt_ctx])
```

You might be asking how you can find a list of USDTs that you can trace. If you have installed the **bcc-tools** package, you can use **tplist-bpfcc -p <pid>** or **tplist-bpfcc -p <path to executable>**, which will print the available USDTs.

The means to add USDT's to an application is very easy. There are libraries in a number of programming languages that allow you to own your own USDTs:

1. Python: **https://pypi.org/project/stapsdt/**

2. Go: **https://github.com/mmcshane/salp**

3. C libstapsdt: **https://github.com/linux-usdt/libstapsdt**

4. Node: **https://www.npmjs.com/package/usdt**

You can see a basic Python example using **stapsdt** that fires a custom probe in your application:

```
import time
import stapsdt

provider = stapsdt.Provider("examplepythonapp")
probe = provider.add_probe(
"firstProbe", stapsdt.ArgTypes.uint64, stapsdt.ArgTypes.
int32)
provider.load()

while True:
        probe.fire("Test USDT", 12345)
        sleep(1)
```

Recommended reading:

• **https://lwn.net/Articles/753601/**

- https://leezhenghui.github.io/linux/2019/03/05/exploring-usdt-on-linux.html

- https://www.collabora.com/news-and-blog/blog/2019/05/14/an-ebpf-overview-part-5-tracing-user-processes/

kprobemulti/ kretprobemulti

Kprobe multi allows the user to attach multiple kprobesin an efficient manner. This allows you to create a regex of kprobesto match against.

For example, if you wanted to have a kprobe fire for every syscall that is initiated (do not do this as it will likely cause performance issues), you could define a kernel-space BPF program that has a wildcard to capture all syscalls :

```
SEC("kprobe.multi/ _sys_*")
int test_kprobe(struct pt_regs *ctx)
{
    unsigned long syscall_nr = PT_REGS_PARM1(ctx);
    bpf_trace_printk(«Syscall Number: %i\n», syscall_nr);
    return 0;
}
```

Overall, the **BPF_PROG_TYPE_KPROBE** is an extremely useful and flexible program type that allows you to instrument nearly all parts of the Linux kernel as well as user-space libraries and program functions.

Tracepoint programs

Tracepoint programs allow you to instrument (pre-defined) tracepoints in kernel code. They can be enabled via sysfs, as is the case with kprobes.

Program type name	BPF_PROG_TYPE_TRACEPOINT
Kernel version introduced	4.7
BPF program context	Per-tracepoint specific context (see more below)
BPF attachment types	N/A
ELF sections	tracepoint/<category>/<name> tp/<category>/<name>

Table 7.2: BPF_PROG_TYPE_TRACEPOINT program attributes

The list of trace events can be seen by listing **/sys/kernel/debug/tracing/events** (you will need to do this as root).

```
$ sudo su
$ ls -l /sys/kernel/debug/tracing/events
total 0
drwxr-x---   6 root root 0 Jun 29 21:18 alarmtimer
drwxr-x---   3 root root 0 Jun 29 21:18 amd_cpu
drwxr-x---  15 root root 0 Jun 29 21:18 asoc
drwxr-x---  13 root root 0 Jun 29 21:18 ath11k
drwxr-x---   3 root root 0 Jun 29 21:18 avc
drwxr-x---  21 root root 0 Jun 29 21:18 block
drwxr-x---   3 root root 0 Jun 29 21:18 bpf_test_run
drwxr-x---   3 root root 0 Jun 29 21:18 bpf_trace
```

You will notice that these are all directories. This is because they are the category of tracepoint. We can go to the next directory level down to see all of the available tracepoints for that category (e.g., **block**).

```
$ ls -l /sys/kernel/debug/tracing/events/block
total 0
drwxr-x--- 2 root root 0 Jun 29 21:18 block_bio_backmerge
drwxr-x--- 2 root root 0 Jun 29 21:18 block_bio_bounce
drwxr-x--- 2 root root 0 Jun 29 21:18 block_bio_complete
drwxr-x--- 2 root root 0 Jun 29 21:18 block_bio_frontmerge
drwxr-x--- 2 root root 0 Jun 29 21:18 block_bio_queue
drwxr-x--- 2 root root 0 Jun 29 21:18 block_bio_remap
drwxr-x--- 2 root root 0 Jun 29 21:18 block_dirty_buffer
drwxr-x--- 2 root root 0 Jun 29 21:18 block_getrq
drwxr-x--- 2 root root 0 Jun 29 21:18 block_plug
...
```

These are the list of tracepoint names for the given category. You will need the category and the name for your **SEC()** declaration in your function. For example:

```
SEC("tracepoint/syscalls/sys_enter_open")
int trace_enter_open(struct syscalls_enter_open_args *ctx)
{
    return 0;
}
```

As we mentioned at the start of the section, the context for a tracepoint program will depend on the event that you are tracing. There is a hard way and an easy way to build the context of your eBPF program argument.

You can **cat** the format of the tracepoint and then create your own custom struct. We will use **syscalls/sys_enter_open** as an example:

```
$ cat /sys/kernel/debug/tracing/events/syscalls/sys_enter_
open/format
name: sys_enter_open
ID: 653
format:
    field:unsigned short common_type;      offset:0;
size:2;     signed:0;
    field:unsigned char common_flags;      offset:2;      size:1;
signed:0;
    field:unsigned char common_preempt_count;      offset:3;
size:1;     signed:0;
    field:int common_pid;      offset:4;      size:4;
signed:1;

    field:int __syscall_nr;      offset:8;      size:4;
signed:1;
    field:const char * filename;      offset:16;      size:8;
signed:0;
    field:int flags;      offset:24;      size:8;      signed:0;
    field:umode_t mode;      offset:32;      size:8;
signed:0;

print fmt: "filename: 0x%08lx, flags: 0x%08lx, mode:
0x%08lx", ((unsigned long)(REC->filename)), ((unsigned
long)(REC->flags)), ((unsigned long)(REC->mode))
```

You can ignore the common fields (these are inaccessible to the BPF program) and focus on the second set of fields. These tell you the name of the tracepoint fields and the size of the field.

```
    field:int __syscall_nr;      offset:8;      size:4;
signed:1;
    field:const char * filename;      offset:16;      size:8;
signed:0;
    field:int flags;      offset:24;      size:8;      signed:0;
    field:umode_t mode;      offset:32;      size:8;
signed:0;
```

This means we have four specific fields:

- `int __syscall_nr`
- `const char * filename`
- `int flags`
- `umode_t mode`

If you have the BCC package installed, the easy way is to use the utility **tplist-bpfcc** which will show you the fields of the tracepoint. Using the tracepoint **syscalls/sys_enter_open** as an example:

```
$ tplist-bpfcc syscalls:sys_enter_open -v
syscalls:sys_enter_open
      int __syscall_nr;
      const char * filename;
      int flags;
      umode_t mode;
```

We can then take these four fields and create a struct **syscalls_enter_open_args**:

```
struct syscalls_enter_open_args {
    int __syscall_nr;
    const char * filename;
    int flags;
    umode_t mode;
}
```

And then use it in our kernel-space BPF program as previously shown in Example 7-9:

Recommended resources:

- **https://lwn.net/Articles/379903/**
- **https://mozillazg.com/2022/05/ebpf-libbpf-tracepoint-common-questions-en.html**
- **https://terenceli.github.io/%E6%8A%80%E6%9C%AF/2020/08/09/ebpf-with-tracepoint**

Raw tracepoint programs

The key difference between a regular tracepoint and raw tracepoints is that a raw tracepoint does not provide a pre-contracted argument struct to the eBPF program in the same manner a regular tracepoint does. The raw tracepoint eBPF program accesses the raw parameters of the tracepoint.

Program type name	BPF_PROG_TYPE_RAW_TRACEPOINT
Kernel version introduced	4.17
BPF program context	`struct bpf_raw_tracepoint_args`
BPF attachment types	N/A
ELF sections	`raw_tp/<name>` `raw_tracepoint/<name>`

Table 7.3: BPF_PROG_TYPE_RAW_TRACEPOINT program attributes

As noted earlier, tracepoints have a stable API. This stability does, however, come with a performance cost. Raw tracepoints are designed to remove the performance penalties of utilizing tracepoints by removing the **TP_fast_assign()** process in the tracepoint execution and allowing access to the arguments of the tracepoint in raw form. Therefore, raw tracepoint has a slightly better performance than a regular tracepoint (see **https://lwn.net/Articles/750569/**).

The argument is a pointer to `struct` **bpf_raw_tracepoint_args**, which is defined in **bpf.h**. The struct field args contains all parameters of the raw tracepoint, which you can find in the Linux **include/ trace/events** directory (each filename corresponds with a tracepoint type).

We recommend reading the following materials for further reading:

- **https://mozillazg.com/2022/05/ebpf-libbpf-raw-tracepoint-common-questions-en.html**

- **https://www.youtube.com/watch?v=h8QMggaqSxI**

Raw tracepoint writeable programs

Raw tracepoint writable programs (building off the raw tracepoint functionality) provide the ability for a tracepoint to predefine a buffer that a **BPF_PROG_TYPE_RAW_TRACEPOINT_WRITEABLE** program can write to when the tracepoint fires. This buffer is the first argument that is accessible by the tracepoint.

Program type name	BPF_PROG_TYPE_RAW_TRACEPOINT_WRITEABLE
Kernel version introduced	5.2
BPF program context	Per-tracepoint specific context (see more below)
BPF attachment types	N/A
ELF sections	raw_tp.w/<name> raw_tracepoint.w/<name>

Table 7.4: BPF_PROG_TYPE_RAW_TRACEPOINT_WRITEABLE
program attributes

The arguments provided by the tracepoint have a writeable context, which allows you to rewrite the data contained in the tracepoint arguments, allowing you to manipulate the behavior of the code after the tracepoint.. The only place where writable tracepoints are currently implemented is in the **Network Block Device (NBD)** tracepoint (**nbd_send_request**), where the buffer is of type **nbd_request**.

Perf event programs

This program type allows you to instrument software and hardware performance events, otherwise known as **perf events**. These include events like syscalls, timer expiry, sampling of hardware events, etc. Hardware events include PMU events (processor monitoring unit), which tell us things like how many instructions were completed, etc.

Program type name	BPF_PROG_TYPE_PERF_EVENT
Kernel version introduced	4.9
BPF program context	struct bpf_perf_event_data
BPF attachment types	N/A
ELF sections	perf_event

Table 7.5: BPF_PROG_TYPE_PERF_EVENT program attributes

The definitions of the Hardware (**enum perf_hw_id**), Software (**enum perf_sw_ids**), and the event sample format (**enum perf_event_sample_format**) can be found **in nclude/uapi/linux/perf_event.h**

Perf event monitoring can be targeted at a specific process or cgroup CPU and a sample period must be specified for profiling. Perf event eBPF programs are triggered by the Linux perf-event sampling condition being triggered.

In BCC, you can directly capture perf events into a **BPF_MAP_TYPE_ PERF_EVENT_ARRAY** map to read within your BPF program using the following syntax:

```
from bcc import BPF, PerfType, PerfSWConfig

num_cpus = len(utils.get_online_cpus())
text="""
BPF_PERF_ARRAY(page_faults, NUM_CPUS);
"""

b = BPF(text=text, cflags=['-DNUM_CPUS=%s' % str(num_cpus)])
b["cpu_cycles"].open_perf_event(PERF_TYPE_HARDWARE, PERF_
COUNT_HW_CPU_CYCLES)
```

This creates a perf array named **cpu_cycles**, with a number of entries equal to the number of CPUs/ cores. The array is configured so that later calling **map.perf_read()** will return a hardware-calculated counter of the number of cycles elapsed from some point in the past. Only one type of hardware counter may be configured per table at a time.

Alternatively, you can attach an eBPF program to the perf event using the following syntax:

```
from bcc import BPF, utils

b = BPF(text=bpf_text)
b.attach_perf_event(
ev_type=PerfType.SOFTWARE, ev_config=PerfHWConfig.PAGE_
FAULTS,
fn_name="on_fault", sample_period=00, sample_freq=1)
```

The code above attaches a perf eBPF program called **on_fault** when a page fault event occurs and triggers the eBPF program. On the kernel side, we create a hash map that contains the PID as the key and increments a counter every time the kernel-space program is invoked by a page fault.

```
#include <uapi/linux/ptrace.h>

BPF_HASH(pfcnt, u32, u64, 10240);

int count_sw_page_faults(struct bpf_perf_event_data *ctx) {
    __u32 pid = bpf_get_current_pid_tgid() >> 32;
    __u64 zero = 0;
    __u64 *count = pfcnt.lookup(&pid);
```

```
    if (count) {
        *count += 1;
    } else {
        pfcnt.update(&pid, &zero);
        count = pfcnt.lookup(&pid);

        if (count) {
            *count += 1;
        }
    }
    return 0;
}
```

You can find more information about capturing perf events on the perf_event_open(2) manpage. You can read more BPF and perf with these resources:

- **https://blogs.oracle.com/linux/post/bpf-a-tour-of-program-types**

- **https://www.brendangregg.com/perf.html#eBPF**

Picking the right program type

In this chapter, we have presented a large number of ways to trace user-space and kernel activities. There are tradeoffs between usability and performance in these different program types. For example, kprobe programs are easier to use, however, they are less efficient than tracepoint or raw tracepoint programs. You should thoroughly evaluate what you are trying to achieve, the stability you require, and how performant your BPF programs need to be.

Conclusion

This chapter provided an introduction into the event tracing functionality that eBPF provides in a relatively simple and flexible manner. It is worth noting that eBPF is a rapidly developing technology and is sometimes under-documented. It is strongly recommended that if you plan to run eBPF on different operating system environments, ensure to thoroughly test your code before attempting a fleet-wide production deployment. In the next chapter, we will talk about the numerous ways that eBPF can be used in networking applications.

CHAPTER 8
eBPF Networking

Introduction

While much of the focus of eBPF has been on observability, the original research was based on *Alexei's* work at Plumgrid in the networking space. This chapter explores the use of eBPF in networking programs.

Structure

In this chapter, we will cover the following topics:

- Introduction to eBPF network programmability
- Socket filters programs
- Traffic Classifiers & Action programs
- XDP programs
- cgroup socket option programs
- cgroup socket programs
- Lightweight tunnel programs
- Segment routing programs
- Socket option programs

- Socket SKB programs
- Socket message programs
- cgroup socket address programs
- Socket reuseport programs
- Flow dissector programs
- Socket lookup programs
- Netfilter programs

Objectives

In this chapter, we will introduce 18 new BPF networking program types and show you how to use each one of them. By the end of the chapter, you should understand the purpose and use of each program type and how to write the corresponding programs.

Introduction to eBPF network programmability

eBPF networking has the following features that make it a desirable platform for providing a software networking data plane:

- **Extensible**: Ability to intercept and manipulate packets from L2-L7. Able to intercept raw packets before they leave the NIC or as soon as they leave the NIC.

- **Fully programmable**: Able to access and program all parts of the network interface/ stack

- **Predictable performance (jitter, delay, throughput)**: Some eBPF programs can run on smart **network interface cards (NICs)** as well as in kernel-space which provides predictable performance.

At the time of writing, there are 18 network related eBPF program types. While some are more adopted than others, the number accurately reflects the flexibility and number of places in the kernel stack where eBPF can be plugged in.

eBPF's adoption across a number of companies has been swift and many hyper-scalers now rely on eBPF programs for their daily operations. The use of eBPF at these companies crosses the following areas of operation:

- Socket filtering
- Load balancing
- DDoS protection
- Network monitoring (flow dissectors)
- Firewalls
- Performance management
- Security monitoring

Application
Socket
BPF_PROG_TYPE_SOCKET_FILTER
BPF_PROG_TYPE_SOCK_OPS
BPF_PROG_TYPE_SK_SKB
BPF_PROG_TYPE_SK_MSG
BPF_PROG_TYPE_SK_REUSEPORT
BPF_PROG_TYPE_SK_LOOKUP
BPF_PROG_TYPE_CGROUP_SKB
BPF_PROG_TYPE_CGROUP_SOCK
BPF_PROG_TYPE_CGROUP_SOCK_ADDR
BPF_PROG_TYPE_CGROUP_SOCKOPT
Netfilter
BPF_PROG_TYPE_NETFILTER
BPF_PROG_TYPE_LWT_IN
BPF_PROG_TYPE_LWT_OUT
BPF_PROG_TYPE_LWT_XMT
BPF_PROG_TYPE_LWT_SEG6LOCAL
TC (traffic control)
BPF_PROG_TYPE_SCHED_CLS
BPF_PROG_TYPE_SCHED_ACT
BPF_PROG_TYPE_XDP (Generic XDP)
Device driver
BPF_PROG_TYPE_XDP (Native XDP)
Network device

Table 8.1: *Illustration of where eBPF networking*
programs operate in the Linux network stack

This chapter will cover all the network-related program types and how to write programs for each of them. Some BPF program types have better documentation than others (especially in the network program space), so utilize the recommended resources as much as possible. Reading through the commit messages does help provide extra context on the intent of the program type. Each program type has a corresponding example application in the GitHub repository.

Socket filter programs

BPF_PROG_TYPE_SOCKET_FILTER was the first eBPF program type created in 2014. It allows you to write programs that run in a similar fashion to cBPF filter programs. You open a socket and filter/trim packets via the filter program, as we demonstrated with cBPF in *Chapter 1, Classic Berkeley Packet Filter*.

Similar to the first applications of cBPF, you can write complex network filters that inspect the full packet before making a decision to accept (return **-1**) or drop the packet (return **0**) back to user-space. It is important to note that packets are not dropped on the system, the original packet will still make it to the original socket/ application unchanged (as compared to a firewall). We are using a copy of the packet, which raw sockets can access for observability. Below are the attributes of the program type:

Program type name	BPF_PROG_TYPE_SOCKET_FILTER
Kernel version introduced	3.19
BPF program context	**struct __sk_buff**
BPF attachment types	N/A
ELF sections	**socket**

Table 8.2: BPF_PROG_TYPE_SOCKET_FILTER properties

The **struct __sk_buff** is given as the BPF program context. This is a data type you will see often in this chapter. **sk_buff** is commonly referred to as a **socket buffer** or **SKB**. In eBPF, we never are able to access the regular **sk_buff** object. The eBPF verifier creates the **struct __sk_buff** object, which has significantly fewer fields as compared to the BPF programs context.

Socket filter programs execute when the **sock_queue_rcv_skb()** function is called by various protocols and can be used to filter inbound traffic. There are two types of return codes for **BPF_PROG_TYPE_SOCKET_FILTER**:

- **0**: DROP the packet

- **-1**: KEEP the packet and return it to user space (user space can read it from an attached socket).

BPF_PROG_TYPE_SOCKET_FILTER programs are attached to sockets using the **SO_ATTACH_BPF** option in **setsockopt()**. When running socket filter programs, we need to attach the filter program to a raw socket on an interface and then read off the socket in the user space program. In a basic sense, this is how programs like **tcpdump** operate.

```
prog_fd = bpf_program__fd(skel->progs.dns_filter);
setsockopt(sock, SOL_SOCKET, SO_ATTACH_BPF, &prog_fd,
sizeof(prog_fd))
```

Similar to what we discussed in *Chapter 1, Classic Berkeley Packet Filter,* eBPF socket filters behave in a similar way to cBPF filters. Here, we demonstrate a very simple socket filter that filters for IP/UDP packets on port 53 and then checks of the packet and then returns the packet (allows it to pass the filter):

```
SEC("socket")
int dns_filter(struct __sk_buff *skb) {
    __u16 eth_type;
    __u8 ip_protocol;
    __u16 udp_dport;

    // Check Ethernet type
    if (bpf_skb_load_bytes(skb, 12, &eth_type, sizeof(eth_
type)) < 0) {
        return 0; // Drop if incomplete
    }
    if (__bpf_ntohs(eth_type) != ETH_P_IP) {
        return 1; // Pass if not IP
    }
    // Check IP protocol
    if (bpf_skb_load_bytes(skb, ETH_HLEN + offsetof(struct
iphdr, protocol), &ip_protocol, sizeof(ip_protocol)) < 0)
{
        return 0; // Drop if incomplete
```

```
    }
    if (ip_protocol != IPPROTO_UDP) {
        return 1; // Pass if not UDP
    }
    // Check UDP destination port
    if (bpf_skb_load_bytes(skb, ETH_HLEN + sizeof(struct
iphdr) /* Assuming no options */ + offsetof(struct udphdr,
dest), &udp_dport, sizeof(udp_dport)) < 0) {
        return 0; // Drop if incomplete
    }
    if (__bpf_ntohs(udp_dport != 53) {
        return 1; // Pass if not DNS port
    }
    return -1;
}
```

This can be paired with a user space application to print information about the received packets (like **tcpdump** does). We will provide an example in (**ch08/ BPF_PROG_TYPE_SOCKET_FILTER**).

We recommend the following supporting resources:

- **https://www.kernel.org/doc/Documentation/networking/ filter.txt** (Note that there are references to cBPF in this article)

- **https://lwn.net/Articles/747551/**

- **https://github.com/iovisor/bcc/tree/master/examples/ networking**

Traffic Classifier programs

The **tc** or Traffic Control subsystem allows the administrator to control how packets are processed by the system. **BPF_PROG_TYPE_SCHED_ CLS** and **BPF_PROG_TYPE_SCHED_ACT** program types work together. We highly recommend you read Introduction to Linux Traffic Control (**https://tldp.org/HOWTO/Traffic   Control-HOWTO/intro.html**) before reading these sections.

Traffic control programs allow you to:

- Prioritize certain types of traffic

- Add artificial latency/packet drops

- Create bandwidth allocations for varying types of packets (i.e. applications)

- Monitor network flows

This is done via manipulating network traffic using four particular concepts of Linux Traffic Control:

- **Shaping**: Shaping controls the rate of transmission. It may do more than just lower the bandwidth available to a stream; it may also be used to smooth out bursty network traffic for more consistent behavior.

- **Scheduling**: By scheduling the egress of packets, it is possible to preserve bandwidth both interactive applications (e.g. webserver) as well as applications that perform bulk transfers of data (e.g. Hadoop).

- **Policing**: Refers to shaping on packet ingress.

- **Dropping**: Network traffic that exceeds a specific bandwidth may be dropped both on ingress and egress.

The processing of network packets is controlled by three kinds of objects: `qdiscs`, `classes` and `filters`.

The eBPF classifier program can also be used in **direct-action** mode, where you can classify and action the traffic within the same program. This simplifies the use of **tc** and avoids indirection and list handling when using the full **tc** action engine. The classifier **classid** can be written in **skb->tc_classid**, and the action opcode (e.g. **TC_ACT_OK**) is returned. Below are the attributes of the program type:

Program type name	BPF_PROG_TYPE_SCHED_CLS
Kernel version introduced	4.1
BPF program context	`struct __sk_buff`
BPF attachment types	N/A
ELF sections	• `classifier` • `tc`

Table 8.3: BPF_PROG_TYPE_SCHED_CLS properties

As mentioned above, a classifier **qdisc** must be created, and then a BPF program must be attached to classify inbound and outbound traffic. Implementation-wise, **net/dev/act_bpf.c** and **net/dev/cls_bpf.c** implement action/classifier modules respectively. On ingress/egress **sch_handle_ingress()/ sch_handle_egress()** in **net/core/ dev.c** call **tcf_classify()**. For ingress traffic, **tc** intercepts it before it has been processed by the IP stack. On egress, filtering is done before the packet is sent to the device queue for transmission. A **BPF_PROG_ TYPE_SCHED_CLS** program has the following return codes:

- **0**: No match found
- **-1**: Default **classid**
- **Any other integer**: Will modify the default **classid** which allows for a packet matching mechanism.

See the **BPF_PROG_TYPE_SCHED_ACT** section for action return code explanations if you are using direct-action mode.

tc(8) can be used to run see **tc-bpf(8)** for details. We can create a **clsact qdisc** for a network device and add ingress and egress classifiers/actions by specifying the BPF object and relevant ELF section that acts on the packet. As an example, to add an ingress classifier:

```
$ tc qdisc add dev <interface> ingress clsact
$ tc filter add dev <interface> ingress bpf obj <bpf object
file> sec tc
```

Classifier programs (without direct-action mode) inspect the contents of the **skb** provided in the context and return an integer that determines the packet **classid**. In this example, we are going to return a **classid** for each TCP port, which can then be used to rate-limit traffic per port:

```
SEC("tc")
int process_packet(struct __sk_buff *skb) {
    struct ethhdr *eth_header;
    struct iphdr *ip_header;
    struct tcphdr *tcp_header;

    if (skb->len < sizeof(struct ethhdr) + sizeof(struct
iphdr)) {
        return -1;
    }
    eth_header = (struct ethhdr *)(long)skb->data;
    ip_header = (struct iphdr *)(long)(skb->data +
sizeof(struct ethhdr));
```

```
    if ((void *)(ip_header + 1) > (void *)(long)skb->data_
end) {
        return -1;
    }

    if (ip_header->protocol == IPPROTO_TCP) {
        tcp_header = (struct tcphdr *)(long)(skb->data +
sizeof(struct ethhdr) + sizeof(struct iphdr));
        return bpf_ntohs(tcp_header->dest); // Return the
destination port
    }
    return -1; // Default return if not TCP
}
```

We recommend the following supporting resources:

- **https://aya-rs.dev/book/programs/classifiers/**
- **https://man7.org/linux/man-pages/man8/tc.8.html**
- **https://man7.org/linux/man-pages/man8/tc-bpf.8.html**
- **https://netdevconf.info/1.1/proceedings/papers/On-getting-tc-classifier-fully-programmable-with-cls-bpf.pdf**
- **https://tldp.org/HOWTO/Traffic Control-HOWTO/intro.html**
- **https://blogs.oracle.com/linux/post/bpf-using-bpf-to-do-packet-transformation**

Traffic classifier action programs

Used with **BPF_PROG_TYPE_SCHED_ACT** program type to take an action on a packet. This may be as simple as allowing the traffic to pass or dropping the packet or as complex as reclassifying it or forcing it to another action program. The following are the attributes of the program type:

Program type name	BPF_PROG_TYPE_SCHED_ACT
Kernel version introduced	4.1
BPF program context	`struct __sk_buff`
BPF attachment types	N/A
ELF sections	`action`

Table 8.4: BPF_PROG_TYPE_SCHED_ACT properties

A **BPF_PROG_TYPE_SCHED_ACT** program has the following return codes:

- **TC_ACT_UNSPEC**   **(-1):** Uses the default action configured from **tc**.

- **TC_ACT_OK (0):** Terminates the packet processing pipeline and allows the packet to proceed.

- **TC_ACT_RECLASSIFY (1):** The classifier returns this code when it wants to reclassify the packet. This means that the packet did not match any of the current classification rules, and the classifier tries a different classification for the packet.

- **TC_ACT_SHOT (2):** This code is returned when the classifier decides to drop the packet. The packet does not proceed any further in the TC pipeline and is discarded (dropped).

- **TC_ACT_PIPE (3):** This return code indicates that the packet should be piped to another action for further processing, such as being sent to another classifier or action in the TC pipeline.

- **TC_ACT_REDIRECT (7):** The classifier program requests the kernel to jump to a different chain or a different classifier for further processing of the packet.

tc(8) can be used; see **tc-bpf(8)** for details on running and loading **tc** BPF programs:

```
$ tc qdisc add dev <interface> clsact
$ tc filter add dev <interface> ingress bpf da obj <bpf
object file> sec action
```

Writing programs

tc action programs are simple in nature as you essentially need to inspect the **skb** context provided and decide what action to take on the packet. For example, if we wanted to write an action that dropped traffic ingress ICMP 7% of the time, we could do the following:

```
SEC("action")
int drop_icmp_randomly(struct __sk_buff *ctx) {
    void *data_end = (void *)(long)ctx->data_end;
    void *data = (void *)(long)ctx->data;
    struct ethhdr *eth = data;
```

```
if (data + sizeof(*eth) > data_end) {
    return TC_ACT_OK;
}

if (eth->h_proto == __bpf_constant_htons(ETH_P_IP)) {
    struct iphdr *ip = data + sizeof(*eth);

    if ((void *)ip + sizeof(*ip) > data_end) {
        return TC_ACT_OK;
    }

    if (ip->protocol == IPPROTO_ICMP) {
        __u32 random_value = bpf_get_prandom_u32();
         if (random_value % 100 < 7) { // Drop with 7%
probability
            bpf_printk("TP3. GOOD");
            return TC_ACT_SHOT;
        }
    }
}
return TC_ACT_OK;
}
```

XDP programs

eXpress Data Path (XDP) programs execute as close as possible to the packet arriving over the wire to the host machine. This removes the need (and bottleneck) of traversing the Linux networking stack, allowing for highly performant and high-throughput load balancing, DDoS, and firewall eBPF programs.

XDP is extremely versatile and is currently being utilized heavily by a number of hyperscale companies as it provides the ability to scale service throughput exponentially while maintaining lower costs. XDP is one of the most well-known eBPF program types (aside from socket filters). It is commonly used in the following ways:

- **Load balancing**: One of the primary use cases of XDP programs is load-balancing. XDP supports either forwarding packets back on the interface on which it was received (**XDP_TX**) or through another network interface (**XDP_REDIRECT**).

- **DDoS mitigation**: Given XDP's early packet processing, it makes it ideal as a DDoS mitigation platform. XDP's **XDP_DROP** action is extremely performant and is ideal for being able to handle a large number of packets without overwhelming the host infrastructure.

- **Firewalls**: Similar to what is mentioned in DDoS Mitigation above, XDP programs can easily assess L3 and L4 packet information and make policy enforcement decisions.

- **Monitoring**: Collecting statistics of your network traffic (at high data rates) can be resource intensive. XDP allows you to efficiently parse packets and increment counters in eBPF maps, bypassing the need to rely on user space.

Below are the attributes of the program type:

Program type name	BPF_PROG_TYPE_XDP
Kernel version introduced	4.8
BPF program context	`struct xdp_md`
BPF attachment types	• `BPF_XDP_CPUMAP` • `BPF_XDP_DEVMAP` • `BPF_XDP`
ELF sections	• `xdp.frags/cpumap` • `xdp/cpumap` • `xdp.frags/devmap` • `xdp/devmap` • `xdp.frags` • `xdp`

Table 8.5: *BPF_PROG_TYPE_XDP properties*

There are three modes for XDP programs. This determines how the program is executed and on what device:

- **Native XDP**: This is the default mode of the XDP program where the program is run in the network card driver's early receive path. Most common 10G **network interface cards** (**NICs**) support this, making XDP preferable over some other network programming frameworks.

- **Offloaded XDP**: This is where the BPF program is offloaded into the NIC, and the program is run on the NIC and not on the host CPU. These NICs are often called SmartNICs as they contain multi-threaded, multicore flow processors that are designed to run these programs in extremely performant manner.

- **Generic XDP**: For drivers that do not support native or offloaded XDP, XDP programs run at a higher point in the Linux networking stack. This is not designed for high-performance situations; it is better suited for testing environments.

By default, the kernel will try to utilize Native XDP, but if it is not supported, it will fall back to generic XDP. We will discuss this more shortly.

The processing of each packet results in one of the following XDP actions being returned in the program:

- **XDP_ABORTED (0):** Drop the packet (program aborted)

- **XDP_DROP (1):** Drop the packet (very fast)

- **XDP_PASS (2):** Pass the packet up the network stack to be processed by the Linux networking stack and any listening application.

- **XDP_TX (3):** Transmit the packet back out the network interface.

- **XDP_REDIRECT (4):** Transmit out through other NICs.

Note: XDP_TX and XDP_REDIRECT were introduced after Linux 4.8.

XDP programs can be loaded using the `ip` command (e.g., `ip link set dev $IFACE xdp obj $XDP_PROG sec xdp`) or can be loaded by using the `bpf_xdp_attach()` libbpf function, which creates a netlink socket message.

Given the popularity of XDP programs (and the many ways they can be used, we will provide some basic examples of each program type. Firstly, let us look at dropping packets:

Imagine running a high-volume publicly facing web-service (i.e. DNS server). This service should be able to accept TCP and UDP packets, but drop other protocols like ping. We can write the following function that checks that we have a valid IP packet and then checks that it is either of UDP or TCP type and then drop everything else:

```
SEC("xdp")
int drop_non_tcp_udp(struct xdp_md *ctx) {
    void *data = (void *)(long)ctx->data;
    void *data_end = (void *)(long)ctx->data_end;

    struct ethhdr *eth = data;
    if (data + sizeof(struct ethhdr) > data_end)
        return XDP_ABORTED;

    if (bpf_ntohs(eth->h_proto) != ETH_P_IP)
        return XDP_DROP;

    struct iphdr *iph = data + sizeof(struct ethhdr);
    if (data + sizeof(struct ethhdr) + sizeof(struct iphdr)
> data_end)
        return XDP_ABORTED;

    if (iph->protocol == IPPROTO_ICMP) {
        return XDP_DROP;
    }
      if (iph->protocol == IPPROTO_TCP || iph->protocol ==
IPPROTO_UDP) {
        return XDP_PASS;
    }
    return XDP_DROP;
}
```

Using XDP, we can also build a simple load balancer that load-balancing inbound UDP/53 packets between two backends. You can find the sample code in **ch08/BPF_PROG_TYPE_XDP/load_balancer**. There is also a reference ICMP ping server code example, which allows the program to be used as a high-performing ICMP network connectivity test. See **ch08/BPF_PROG_TYPE_XDP/icmp_server**.

We recommend the following supporting resources:

- **https://github.com/xdp-project/xdp-tutorial**
- **https://blogs.oracle.com/linux/post/the-power-of-xdp**
- **https://www.kernel.org/doc/html/latest/networking/af_xdp. html**
- **https://aya-rs.dev/book/start/hello-xdp/**

- https://developers.redhat.com/blog/2018/12/06/achieving-high-performance-low-latency-networking-with-xdp-part-1/

- https://netdevconf.info/2.1/slides/apr6/zhou-netdev-xdp-2017.pdf

cgroup socket programs

BPF_PROG_TYPE_CGROUP_SOCK programs are executed when a program within a defined cgroup either opens a socket, binds, or releases a socket.

You use the provided context to check for certain conditions relating to the socket created, binded, released (e.g. family) and then either allow or deny access. You could use this as a security mechanism to only allow very specific protocols when creating sockets. This provides benefits over always-on packet processing. This allows you to set broad security and access control restrictions over the cgroup. The following are the attributes of the program type:

Program type name	BPF_PROG_TYPE_CGROUP_SOCK
Kernel version introduced	4.10
BPF program context	`struct bpf_sock`
BPF attachment types	• `BPF_CGROUP_INET4_POST_BIND` • `BPF_CGROUP_INET6_POST_BIND` • `BPF_CGROUP_INET_SOCK_CREATE` • `BPF_CGROUP_INET_SOCK_RELEASE`
ELF sections	• `cgroup/post_bind4` • `cgroup/post_bind6` • `cgroup/sock_create` • `cgroup/sock` • `cgroup/sock_release`

Table 8.6: BPF_PROG_TYPE_CGROUP_SOCK properties

BPF_PROG_TYPE_CGROUP_SOCK programs run when one of the following conditions is met (based on the program attach type):

- At socket creation time
- At socket bind time
- At socket bind
- At socket release time

BPF_PROG_TYPE_CGROUP_SOCK programs return the following error codes:

- **0**: Block traffic
- **1**: Let the socket event complete (create, bind, close)

The program is attached to the cgroup's file descriptor. For example:

```
$ bpftool prog load <bpf object file> /sys/fs/bpf/your_
program_name
$ bpftool cgroup attach /path/to/cgroup1/ your_program_name
```

BPF_PROG_TYPE_CGROUP_SOCK programs are fairly simple to write. The following example blocks and IPv4 ICMP socket creation, but allows everything else:

```
SEC("cgroup/sock_create")
int block_v4_icmp(struct bpf_sock *ctx)
{
    // block PF_INET, SOCK_RAW, IPPROTO_ICMP sockets
    if (ctx->family == AF_INET &&
        ctx->type == SOCK_DGRAM    &&
        ctx->protocol == IPPROTO_ICMP)
        return 0;
    return 1;
}
```

We recommend the following supporting resources:

- **https://www.alibabacloud.com/blog/improving-kubernetes-service-network-performance-with-socket-ebpf_599446**

Lightweight tunnel programs

Lightweight tunnels allow you to attach encapsulation (e.g., **Multiprotocol Label Switching** (MPLS) or **Generic Routing Encapsulation** (GRE)) to routes. This helps with scaling tunnel endpoints by eliminating tunnel net devices using LWT and flow-based tunnels. **LWT_IN/LWT_OUT** programs are able to read the data in the **sk_buff** context but do not make any modifications. **LWT_XMIT** programs are able to modify packet content as well as prepend a Layer 2 header (i.e. MPLS). Below are the attributes of the program type:

Program type name	BPF_PROG_TYPE_LWT_IN/BPF_PROG_TYPE_LWT_OUT/BPF_PROG_TYPE_LWT_XMIT
Kernel version introduced	4.10
BPF program context	`struct sk_buff * skb`
BPF attachment types	N/A
ELF sections	• `lwt_in` • `lwt_out` • `lwt_xmit`

Table 8.7: BPF_PROG_TYPE_LWT_* properties

LWT eBPF programs are executed as hooks in the following scenarios:

- **LWT_IN**: Examine inbound packets
- **LWT_OUT**: Examine outbound packets

  LWT_XMIT: Implement encapsulation/redirection for lightweight tunnels on transmit

See *Traffic classifier action programs* section for valid program return codes.

LWT programs are loaded using the **ip route** command.

- **LWT_IN**: `ip route add 10.0.0.2/32 encap bpf in obj <bpf object file> section lwt_in dev <interface>`
- **LWT_OUT**: `ip route add 10.0.0.2/32 encap bpf out obj <bpf object file> section lwt_out dev <interface>`
- **LWT_XMIT**: `ip route add 10.0.0.2/32 encap bpf xmit obj <bpf object file> section lwt_xmit dev <interface>`

There are two categories of programs that can be written here. First, for **LWT_IN**/**LWT_OUT**, where you can inspect the packets. This example **LWT_IN** program sums the length of the packets being received over the tunnel and groups them by protocol:

```
struct {
    __uint(type, BPF_MAP_TYPE_HASH);
    __uint(key_size, sizeof(__u8));
    __uint(value_size, sizeof(__u64));
    __uint(max_entries, 256); // Assuming protocol numbers
are within 0-255
```

```
} protocol_counts SEC(".maps");
SEC("lwt_in")
int count_protocols(struct __sk_buff *skb) {
    void *data_end = (void *)(long)skb->data_end;
    void *data = (void *)(long)skb->data;
    __u8 protocol = 0;

    if (skb->protocol == __bpf_constant_htons(ETH_P_IP)) {
        struct iphdr *iph = data;
        if (data + sizeof(struct ethhdr) + sizeof(struct
iphdr) > data_end) {
            return BPF_OK;
        }
        protocol = iph->protocol;
    } else {
        return BPF_OK;
    }

    __u64 *count = bpf_map_lookup_elem(&protocol_counts,
&protocol);
    if (count) {
        (*count)++;
    } else {
        __u64 initial_count = 1;
        bpf_map_update_elem(&protocol_counts, &protocol,
&initial_count, BPF_ANY);
    }
    return BPF_OK;
}
```

In the **LWT_XMIT** program type, you can rewrite the **skb** and also redirect the packet to a different interface. You can find this example in **ch08/BPF_PROG_TYPE_LWT_XMIT** of the GitHub repository.

We recommend the following supporting resources:

- **https://lwn.net/Articles/650778/**

- **https://netdevconf.info/1.1/proceedings/slides/ahern-aleksandrov-prabhu-scaling-network-cumulus.pdf**

- **https://github.com/fzakaria/ebpf-mpls-encap-decap/**

Segment routing programs

Segment routing is a network protocol that allows the sender of a packet to specify a route for the packet through a series of segments (hops) within the network. In the case of **Seg6Local**, the segments are defined locally on the host itself, and the host can process packets based on those segments.

This program type is used for processing packets in the context of **Seg6Local** processing. It is attached to the local processing engine of the Linux kernel's Segment Routing implementation. **Seg6Local** enables you to define segments on the local host itself and steer packets through those segments using a **Segment Routing Header** (SRH).

When a packet with an SRH arrives at the local host, the **Seg6Local** BPF program can be used to make decisions about how to handle the packet based on the segments in the SRH. This can include forwarding, modifying, or otherwise processing the packet based on your application's requirements. The following are the attributes of the program type:

Program type name	BPF_PROG_TYPE_LWT_SEG6LOCAL
Kernel version introduced	4.18
BPF program context	`struct __sk_buff`
BPF attachment types	N/A
ELF sections	`lwt_seg6local`

Table 8.8: BPF_PROG_TYPE_LWT_SEG6LOCAL properties

A **Seg6Local** BPF program must return one of the three following return values. These values indicate to **End.BPF** the final step of the SRv6 processing that must be applied on the packet:

- **BPF_OK**: Proceed to look up the next destination through `seg6_lookup_nexthop()`.

- **BPF_REDIRECT**: If an action has been executed through the `bpf_lwt_seg6_action()` helper, the BPF program should return this value.

- **BPF_DROP**: Drop the packet.

Similarly to the other Lightweight Tunnel program types, **Seg6Local** programs are attached by using ip route:

```
$ ip -6 route add dead::beef encap seg6local action End.
BPF endpoint object <bpf object file> section my_function
dev <interface>
```

Every instance of an **End.BPF** action is attached to a given eBPF program. It advances the SRH to the next segment, which then executes the associated eBPF code. IPv6 packets containing an SRH with **Segments Left > 0** are accepted. **Segments Left** is then decremented, and the next segment to be processed is copied to the IPv6 Destination Address field by the action before the next eBPF program is executed.

There are a number of different ways **LWT_SEG6LOCAL** program can be used. For our example, we will add SRH's to the packet:

```
SEC("lwt_seg6local")
int encap_srh(struct __sk_buff *skb)
{
    uint64_t hi = 0xfd00000000000000;
    struct ip6_addr_t *seg;
    struct ip6_srh_t *srh;
    char srh_buf[72]; // room for 4 segments
    int err;

    srh = (struct ip6_srh_t *)srh_buf;
    srh->nexthdr = 0;
    srh->hdrlen = 8;
    srh->type = 4;
    srh->segments_left = 3;
    srh->first_segment = 3;
    srh->flags = 0;
    srh->tag = 0;

    seg = (struct ip6_addr_t *)((char *)srh + sizeof(*srh));

    #pragma clang loop unroll(full)
    for (uint64_t lo = 0; lo < 4; lo++) {
        seg->lo = bpf_cpu_to_be64(4 - lo);
        seg->hi = bpf_cpu_to_be64(hi);
      seg = (struct ip6_addr_t *)((char *)seg + sizeof(*seg));
    }

    err = bpf_lwt_push_encap(skb, 0, (void *)srh, sizeof(srh_
buf));
```

```
if (err) {
    return BPF_DROP;
}
return BPF_REDIRECT;
}
```

Other ways you can use this program type is to add and remove TLV's from an SRH and add or remove tags. See **tools/testing/ selftests/bpf/progs/test_lwt_seg6local.c** for further detailed examples.

We recommend the following supporting resources:

- **https://segment-routing.org/index.php/Implementation/BPF**

- **https://segment-routing.org/index.php/Implementation/ AdvancedConf**

- **https://github.com/Zashas/Thesis-SRv6-BPF**

- **https://www.segment-routing.net/images/20221024-srv6-network-programming-netdev.pdf**

Socket option programs

BPF_PROG_TYPE_SOCK_OPS programs allow you to modify socket connection options (sockops) at runtime. This allows you to modify the options of a socket at various stages of the kernel networking stack without needing to modify any source-code. This method has an advantage over other mechanisms like sysctl's, route-metrics, and **setsockopts()**, as it provides programmability on a per-socket basis.

As an example, *Facebook* uses it to set a short **recovery time objective** (**RTO**) for connections between hosts within the same data center (see **samples/bpf/tcp_clamp_kern.c** in the kernel source). The following are the attributes of the program type:

Program type name	BPF_PROG_TYPE_SOCK_OPS
Kernel version introduced	4.13
BPF program context	**struct bpf_sock_ops**
BPF attachment types	**BPF_CGROUP_SOCK_OPS**
ELF sections	**sockops**

Table 8.9: BPF_PROG_TYPE_SOCK_OPS properties

Sockops programs can be triggered at different parts of the Linux networking stack. BPF programs use the op field of the program context variable to indicate the context to act on. There are two types of sockops operations:

- Effect is made through the return value of the BPF program.
- Effect is made using the **bpf_setsocketopt()** BPF helper function.

Some examples of operands of the first type are:
- **BPF_SOCKET_OPS_TIMEOUT_INIT**
- **BPF_SOCKET_OPS_RWND_INIT**
- **BPF_SOCKET_OPS_NEEDS_ECN**

Some examples of operands of the second type are:
- **BPF_SOCKET_OPS_TCP_CONNECT_CB**
- **BPF_SOCKET_OPS_ACTIVE_ESTABLISHED_CB**
- **BPF_SOCKET_OPS_PASSIVE_ESTABLISHED_CB**

You can find the full list of conditions where a sockops program can be used in **bpf.h**.

A **BPF_PROG_TYPE_SOCK_OPS** program has the following return codes:

- **< 0**: Something went wrong
- **0**: The kernel will change this to be the **sk->reply** value
- **1**: The default return value.

The basic premise of this type of program is that you intercept the particular socket event you are looking for and then execute your code. The following example program runs when the **BPF_SOCK_OPS_TCP_CONNECT_CB** operation is hit and modified to send and receive buffer size to **30000** bytes:

```
SEC("sockops")
int modify_buffers(struct bpf_sock_ops *skops) {
    int bufsize = 30000;
    int rv = 0;
    int op;
    op = (int) skops->op;

    switch (op) {
        case BPF_SOCK_OPS_TCP_CONNECT_CB:
```

```
        case BPF_SOCK_OPS_PASSIVE_ESTABLISHED_CB:
            rv = bpf_setsockopt(skops, SOL_SOCKET, SO_SNDBUF,
&bufsize, sizeof(bufsize));
            rv += bpf_setsockopt(skops, SOL_SOCKET, SO_RCVBUF,
&bufsize, sizeof(bufsize));
            break;
        default:
            rv = -1;
        }
    skops->reply = rv;
    return 1;
}
```

We recommend the following supporting resources:

- **https://lwn.net/Articles/725722/**

- **https://cyral.com/blog/how-to-ebpf-accelerating-cloud-native/**

- **https://github.com/zachidan/ebpf-sockops**

Socket SKB programs

BPF_PROG_TYPE_SK_SKB is a special kind of eBPF program that attaches to a socket map (**BPF_MAP_TYPE_SOCKMAP**) that allows you to pipe/forward data between TCP sockets using socket redirects all inside of kernel-space using eBPF (avoiding user-space). This allows you to create very efficient L7 load balancing proxies. Cillium and Facebook's Katran use this type of program extensively for load balancing. The following are the attributes of the program type:

Program type name	BPF_PROG_TYPE_SK_SKB
Kernel version introduced	4.14
BPF program context	`struct __sk_buff`
BPF attachment types	• `BPF_SK_SKB_STREAM_PARSER` • `BPF_SK_SKB_STREAM_VERDICT`
ELF sections	• `sk_skb` • `sk_skb/stream_parser` • `sk_skb/stream_verdict`

Table 8.10: BPF_PROG_TYPE_SK_SKB properties

The use of the **BPF_PROG_TYPE_SK_SKB** program type happens in three steps:

- A stream parser can be attached to a socket via **BPF_SK_SKB_STREAM_PARSER** attachment to a sockmap, and the parser runs on socket receive on **sk_psock_strp_read()**.

- **BPF_SK_SKB_STREAM_VERDICT** program type attaches to the sockmap and is run on **sk_psock_verdict_recv()**.

- The socket redirection happens via **sk_redirect_map()** or **sk_redirect_hash()** depending on if you are using a **BPF_MAP_TYPE_SOCKMAP** or **BPF_MAP_TYPE_SOCKHASH,** respectively.

A **BPF_PROG_TYPE_SK_SKB** parser program has the following return codes:

- **> 0**: This is the length of a successfully parsed message

- **0**: More data must be received to parse the message

- **-ESTRPIPE**: The current message should not be processed by the kernel; return control of the socket to user space.

A **BPF_PROG_TYPE_SK_SKB** verdict program has the following return codes:

- SK_DROP (0) on error

- SK_PASS (1) on success

The strparser program is attached via **BPF_SK_SKB_STREAM_PARSER** attachment type and should return the length of data parsed. The redirection program is attached to a sockmap as **BPF_SK_SKB_STREAM_VERDICT** attachment type and should return the result of **bpf_sk_redirect_map()**.

In this example, we will implement a simple proxy that forwards traffic based on the incoming port number. The first program you need to create is a stream parser program. This program will determine the length of the next message in the stream. This is as simple as:

```
SEC("sk_skb/stream_parser")
int bpf_prog_parser(struct __sk_buff *skb) {
    return skb->len;
}
```

The second program is the verdict program, which picks a socket to redirect the incoming packets. This program has a SOCKMAP with 65535 entries (which represents a destination port number), and you can insert a listening socket into the map corresponding to a backend listening server:

```
struct {
__uint(type, BPF_MAP_TYPE_SOCKMAP);
__uint(max_entries, 65535);
__type(key, __u32);
__type(value, __u64);
} socket_map SEC(".maps");

SEC("sk_skb/stream_verdict")
int stream_verdict_prog(struct __sk_buff *skb)
{
    _u32 idx = bpf_htonl(skb->local_port) >> 16;
    return bpf_sk_redirect_map(skb, &socket_map, idx, 0);
}
```

You can refer to the full example at **ch08/BPF_PROG_TYPE/BPF_PROG_TYPE_SK_SKB** in the GitHub repository.

We recommend the following supporting resources:

- https://github.com/jsitnicki/srecon-2023-sockmap/blob/main/sockmap-cheatsheet.png
- https://github.com/jsitnicki/sockmap-project/
- https://lwn.net/Articles/731133/
- http://vger.kernel.org/lpc_net2018_talks/ktls_bpf_paper.pdf
- https://docs.kernel.org/bpf/map_sockmap.html
- https://www.kernel.org/doc/Documentation/networking/strparser.txt
- https://lwn.net/Articles/748628/
- https://blog.cloudflare.com/sockmap-tcp-splicing-of-the-future/
- https://GitHub.com/dbolcsfoldi/ebpf-spice-cookie.git

Socket message programs

The **BPF_PROG_TYPE_SK_MSG** program type allows you to control whether a message (**sendmsg()/ sendpage()**) sent to a socket should be allowed/delivered. This allows you to do a deep inspection of traffic (or perform kernel TLS). You can also redirect traffic to a specific socket if needed. Below are the attributes of the program type:

Program type name	BPF_PROG_TYPE_SK_MSG
Kernel version introduced	4.17
BPF program context	struct sk_msg_md
BPF attachment types	BPF_SK_MSG_VERDICT
ELF sections	sk_msg

Table 8.11: *BPF_PROG_TYPE_SK_MSG properties*

This program runs any time the **sendmsg()** or **sendpage()** system calls are executed when writing to a socket. This allows you to perform policy enforcement and monitoring of data at the socket layer.

The **BPF_PROG_TYPE_SK_MSG** program returns either one of two values:

- **SK_DROP (0)**: Frees the copied data in the **sendmsg()** case and in the **sendpage()** case leaves the data untouched. Both cases return **-EACESS** to the user.

- **SK_PASS (1)**: Will allow the message to be sent.

The program executes upon a **sendmsg()/sendpage()** call on a socket and must be attached to a socket map (**BPF_MAP_TYPE_SOCKMAP** or **BPF_MAP_TYPE_SOCKHASH**):

```
$ bpftool prog load <bpf object file> /sys/fs/bpf/bpf_sk_msg
map name sock_ops_map pinned /sys/fs/bpf/sock_ops_map
$ bpftool prog attach pinned /sys/fs/bpf/bpf_sk_msg msg_
verdict pinned sys/fs/bpf/sock_ops_map
```

Once the map has the program attached, all the sockets in the map object inherit the program which gets executed upon any **sendmsg()/ sendpage()** calls to the socket.

The following example blocks traffic destined for port 80, but allows all other ports except for 1337 which is redirected using the socket map (at index 0). You can use a sockops program to populate the attached sockmap with the appropriate socket references (see **ch08/BPF_PROG_ TYPE_SK_MSG** for more):

```
struct {
    __uint(type, BPF_MAP_TYPE_SOCKMAP);
    __uint(key_size, sizeof(uint32_t));
    __uint(value_size, sizeof(uint64_t));
    __uint(max_entries,1);
} sk_redirect_map SEC(".maps");

SEC("sk_msg")
int prog_msg_verdict(struct sk_msg_md *msg) {
    __u32 rport = msg->remote_port;
    if (rport == 80) {
        return SK_DROP; //Don't allow HTTP traffic
    }
    if (rport != 1337) {
        return SK_PASS; // Allow all other traffic to pass
except port 1337
    }
    bpf_msg_redirect_map(msg, &sk_redirect_map, 0, BPF_F_
INGRESS);
    return SK_PASS;
}
```

We recommend the following supporting resources:

- **https://github.com/jsitnicki/kubecon-2024-sockmap/blob/ main/cheatsheet-sockmap-redirect.png**

- **https://github.com/jsitnicki/srecon-2023-sockmap**

- **https://git.kernel.org/pub/scm/ linux/kernel/git/torvalds/linux.git/ commit/?id=4f738adba30a7cfc006f605707e7aee847ffefa**

- **https://cyral.com/blog/how-to-ebpf-accelerating-cloud- native/**

cgroup socket address programs

The **BPF_PROG_TYPE_CGROUP_SOCK_ADDR** program type allows you to intercept and manipulate the IP addresses and port numbers used by user-space applications in a specific cgroup. This ensures that all incoming and outgoing connections to these applications use the IP and port provided by the BPF program.

If a cgrouped process should use a specific IP address on the underlying host with multiple IP addresses configured, the SOCK_ADDR program type allows TCP/UDP applications to be bound to a specific IP/port for all ingress/egress connections.

You will need to run separate programs for IPv4 and IPv6 address families. Below are the attributes of the program type:

Program type name	BPF_PROG_TYPE_CGROUP_SOCK_ADDR
Kernel version introduced	4.17
BPF program context	**struct bpf_sock_addr**
BPF attachment types	• **BPF_CGROUP_INET4_BIND** • **BPF_CGROUP_INET4_CONNECT** • **BPF_CGROUP_INET4_GETPEERNAME** • **BPF_CGROUP_INET4_GETSOCKNAME** • **BPF_CGROUP_INET6_BIND** • **BPF_CGROUP_INET6_CONNECT** • **BPF_CGROUP_INET6_GETPEERNAME** • **BPF_CGROUP_INET6_GETSOCKNAME** • **BPF_CGROUP_UDP4_RECVMSG** • **BPF_CGROUP_UDP4_SENDMSG** • **BPF_CGROUP_UDP6_RECVMSG** • **BPF_CGROUP_UDP6_SENDMSG**
ELF sections	• **cgroup/bind4** • **cgroup/connect4** • **cgroup/getpeername4** • **cgroup/getsockname4** • **cgroup/bind6** • **cgroup/connect6** • **cgroup/getpeername6** • **cgroup/getsockname6** • **cgroup/recvmsg4** • **cgroup/sendmsg4** • **cgroup/recvmsg6** • **cgroup/sendmsg6**

Table 8.12: BPF_PROG_TYPE_CGROUP_SOCK_ADDR properties

The following system calls are made within a cgroup when the program is loaded:

- bind4/bind6
- connect4/connect6
- getpeername4/getpeername6
- getsockname4/getsockname6
- UDP recvmsg4/recvmsg6
- UDP sendmsg4/sendmsg6

A **BPF_PROG_TYPE_CGROUP_SOCK_ADDR** returns the following values:

- **0**: Permission denied, or the socket family is not AF_INET or AF_INET6.
- **1**: Program success, action allowed.

Programs are attached to a particular cgroup using the cgroup's file descriptor:

```
$ bpftool prog load <bpf object file> /sys/fs/bpf/your_
program_name
$ bpftool cgroup attach /path/to/your/cgroup sock_addr
your_program_name
```

The **BPF_PROG_TYPE_CGROUP_SOCK_ADDR** program type can be used in multiple ways. In this example, we will implement a program that intercepts **bind()** and only allows IPv4/ TCP sockets to be bound:

```
SEC("cgroup/bind4")
int bind_v4_prog(struct bpf_sock_addr *ctx)
{
    struct bpf_sock *sk;
    sk = ctx->sk;
    if (!sk)
        return 0;
    if (sk->family != AF_INET)
        return 0;
    if (ctx->type != SOCK_STREAM)
        return 0;
    return 1;
}
```

There are also four other ways you can utilize the **BPF_PROG_TYPE_CGROUP_SOCK_ADDR** program type. We will provide examples in the GitHub repository (**ch08/BPF_PROG_TYPE_CGROUP_SOCK_ADDR**):

- **Connect**: Rewrite any outbound connection destined for port 53 to port 5353.
- **Getsockname**: Intercepts **getsockname()** and rewrites local port 6000 to 1.2.3.4:60001.
- **Recvmsg**: Intercepts the **recvmsg()** call and rewrites the destination port to 192.168.1.53:5000.
- **Sendmsg**: Intercepts the **sendmsg()** call and rewrites the source and destination IP and ports.

We recommend the following supporting resources:

- **https://github.com/torvalds/linux/commit/4fbac77d2d092b475dda9eea66da674369665427**
- **https://ostconf.com/system/attachments/files/000/001/702/original/Dmitry_Krivenok_Linux_networking_in_enterprise_storage.pdf?1570438244**

Socket reuseport programs

The **BPF_PROG_TYPE_SK_REUSEPORT** program type allows you to place a set of application sockets configured with **SO_REUSEPORT** in a BPF map (**BPF_MAP_TYPE_REUSEPORT_SOCKARRAY**) and then utilize the BPF program to pick which socket should serve the incoming connection. This program type is also helpful for migrating connections between an old and new server (e.g., during deployment) or to perform specific A/B testing between server processes. The following are the attributes of the program type:

Program type name	BPF_PROG_TYPE_SK_REUSEPORT
Kernel version introduced	4.19
BPF program context	`struct sk_reuseport_md`
BPF attachment types	• `BPF_SK_REUSEPORT_SELECT_OR_MIGRATE` • `BPF_SK_REUSEPORT_SELECT`
ELF sections	• `sk_reuseport/migrate` • `sk_reuseport`

Table 8.13: BPF_PROG_TYPE_SK_REUSEPORT properties

A **BPF_PROG_TYPE_SK_REUSEPORT** program returns either:

- **SK_DROP (0)**: Disallow the reuse of a port by a program.

- **SK_PASS (1)**: Allow the kernel to pick the reuse port selected using **bpf_sk_select_reuseport()**.

You will need to create a **REUSEPORT_SOCKARRAY** map before you load and attach your reuseport program:

```
# Create a BPF map of type BPF_MAP_TYPE_REUSEPORT_SOCKARRAY
bpftool map create reuseport_sockarray BPF_MAP_TYPE_
REUSEPORT_SOCKARRAY 1024
bpftool prog load <bpf object file> /sys/kernel/bpf/prog/
sk_reuseport
bpftool prog attach /sys/kernel/bpf/prog/sk_reuseport
reuseport_sockarray
```

In this example, we will show two different servers running on the same host using port TCP/8888 (using **SO_REUSEPORT**) and the BPF program picking which server to send the packets to based the source port number.

In this setup, we can assume two servers on the same host both bound to port TCP/8888 using the **SO_REUSEPORT** option. If the source port is below 32000, the traffic will be destined for server instance one, otherwise sent to server instance two. These are inserted into the **REUSEPORT_SOCKARRAY** map (**reuse_array**) as index 0 and 1 respectively.

```
SEC("sk_reuseport")
int select_sock(struct sk_reuseport_md *ctx) {
    void *data_end = (void *)(long)ctx->data_end;
    void *data = (void *)(long)ctx->data;
    if (ctx->ip_protocol == IPPROTO_TCP) {
        struct tcphdr *tcp = data;
        if ((void *)(tcp + 1) > data_end) {
            return SK_PASS;
        }
        __u16 src_port = bpf_ntohs(tcp->source);
        if (src_port < 32000) {
            int server_instance_1 = 0;
            bpf_sk_select_reuseport(ctx, &reuseport_array,
```

```
&server_instance_1, 0);
        return SK_PASS;
    } else {
        int server_instance_2 = 1;
        bpf_sk_select_reuseport(ctx, &reuseport_array,
&server_instance_2, 0);
        return SK_PASS;
    }
}
    return SK_PASS;
}
```

We recommend the following supporting resources:

- **https://lwn.net/ml/netdev/20180808075917.3009181-1-kafai@ fb.com/**

- **https://linuxplumbersconf.org/event/4/contributions/487/ attachments/238/417/Programmable_socket_lookup_ LPC_19.pdf**

- **https://lwn.net/Articles/542629/**

Flow dissector programs

BPF_PROG_TYPE_FLOW_DISSECTOR programs are designed to hook the kernel's flow-dissector and allow you to write a custom flow-dissector using the benefits of BPF. The kernel needs to process packet headers but not fully process the packet; it is considered dissected. This happens regularly in the **tc** subsystem. The following are the attributes of the program type:

Program type name	BPF_PROG_TYPE_FLOW_DISSECTOR
Kernel version introduced	4.20
BPF program context	`struct __sk_buff`
BPF attachment types	`BPF_FLOW_DISSECTOR`
ELF sections	`flow_dissector`

Table 8.14: BPF_PROG_TYPE_FLOW_DISSECTOR properties

BPF flow dissector programs are provided a modified **struct __ sk_buff** as program context. Only these fields are accessible: **data,**

data_end and **flow_keys**. **flow_keys** is struct of **bpf_flow_keys** and contains flow dissector input and output arguments. Flow dissection programs are run during **__skb_flow_dissect()** in **net/core/flow_dissector.c**.

The return code of the BPF program is either:

- **BPF_OK** (0) to indicate successful dissection
- **BPF_DROP** (2) to indicate parsing error.
- **BPF_FLOW_DISSECTOR_CONTINUE** (129):No custom dissection was performed, and fallback to standard kernel dissector is requested.

In the following example, we intercept **Open Shortest Path First** (**OSPF**) routing packets (which isn't supported by the Linux dissector) and implement some custom dissection logic, if the packet isn't OSPF, then we let the default dissector continue dissecting the packet.

```
SEC("flow_dissector")
int flow_dissect(struct __sk_buff *skb)
{
    struct bpf_flow_keys *keys = skb->flow_keys;
    if (keys->n_proto == bpf_htons(ETH_P_IP)) {
        struct iphdr *iph, _iph;
        struct tcphdr *tcp, _tcph;
        struct udphdr *udp, _udph;

        iph = bpf_flow_dissect_get_header(skb, sizeof(*iph), &_iph);
        if (!iph) {
            return BPF_FLOW_DISSECTOR_CONTINUE;
        if (iph->protocol == 89) {
            // Custom OSPF dissection logic
        }
        return BPF_FLOW_DISSECTOR_CONTINUE
    }
}
```

We recommend the following supporting resources:

- **https://www.kernel.org/doc/html/latest/bpf/prog_flow_dissector.html**
- **https://lwn.net/Articles/764200/**

- **https://netdevconf.info/0x15/slides/16/Flow%20dissector_PANDA%20parser.pdf**

cgroup socket option programs

BPF_PROG_TYPE_CGROUP_SOCKOPT programs are executed during **setsockopt()** and **getsockopt()** system calls and allow changing the provided arguments. You can use the program in the following ways depending on the attachment type:

1. **BPF_CGROUP_GETSOCKOPT**: This BPF hook can view the kernel-returned **optval, optlen** and **retval** before sending it to user-space. The BPF program can modify the **optval** and **optlen** and reset **retval** to 0.

2. **BPF_CGROUP_SETSOCKOPT**: This gives a writable context and can modify the supplied arguments to **setsockopt()** before pushing them down to the kernel.

The following are the attributes of the program type:

Program type name	BPF_PROG_TYPE_CGROUP_SOCKOPT
Kernel version introduced	5.3
BPF program context	**struct bpf_sockopt**
BPF attachment types	• **BPF_CGROUP_GETSOCKOPT** • **BPF_CGROUP_SETSOCKOPT**
ELF sections	• **cgroup/getsockopt** • **cgroup/setsockopt**

Table 8.15: BPF_PROG_TYPE_CGROUP_SOCKOPT properties

BPF_PROG_TYPE_CGROUP_SOCKOPT programs are triggered in one of two ways:

- **BPF_CGROUP_GETSOCKOPT**: Called each time a process executes the **getsockopt()** system call.

- **BPF_CGROUP_SETSOCKOPT**: Called each time a process executes the **setsockopt()** system call.

The program return codes are as follows:

- **0**: Deny the system call

- **1**:

o **getsockopt()**: Success: Continue with the next BPF program in the cgroup chain.

o **setsockopt()**: Success: Copies **optval** and **optlen** to userspace and returns **retval** from the system call.

Sock-op programs require you to parse the option level (i.e **SOL_IP** or **SOL_UDP**) and the option name (i.e. **IP_FREEBIND, IP_TOS**). The available options are defined in **include/linux/socket.h** and **include/uapi/linux/in.h** respectively:

```
SEC("cgroup/setsockopt")
int setsockopt_handler(struct bpf_sockopt *ctx) {
    bpf_printk("setsockopt called: level=%d, optname=%d\n",
ctx->level, ctx->optname);

    // Allow SO_RCVBUF (socket receive buffer size)
    if (ctx->optname == SO_RCVBUF) {
        bpf_printk("Allowing SO_RCVBUF setsockopt
call.\n");
        return 1; // Allow
    }
    // Deny SO_DEBUG (debugging option)
    if (ctx->optname == SO_DEBUG) {
        bpf_printk("Blocking SO_DEBUG setsockopt call.\n");
        return 0; // Deny
    }
    return 1; // Allow all other options by default
}
```

We recommend the following supporting resources:

* https://www.kernel.org/doc/html/latest/bpf/prog_cgroup_sockopt.html

Socket lookup programs

The **BPF_PROG_TYPE_SK_LOOKUP** program type allows you to bypass the traditional limitations of the **bind()** system call to select a specific listening socket for new incoming TCP connections or an unconnected socket for UDP packets. Usually, the kernel would know what IP address and ports sockets are bound on, however, this program type allows the user to overring the kernel's method of assigning connections.

The BPF **sk_lookup** program type was created to work around the traditional limitations of the **bind()** system call, for example:

- Receiving connections for a whole /24 (e.g. 1.1.1.0/24) to a single socket (bind only allows you to listen on a specific IP or a wildcard, not IP ranges).

- Receiving connections destined for one IP address on all or a large number of ports and forwarding to a particular socket (e.g. L7 proxy).

Below are the attributes of the program type:

Program type name	BPF_PROG_TYPE_SK_LOOKUP
Kernel version introduced	5.9
BPF program context	**struct bpf_sk_lookup**
BPF attachment types	**BPF_SK_LOOKUP**
ELF sections	**sk_lookup**

Table 8.16: BPF_PROG_TYPE_SK_LOOKUP properties

sk_lookup programs run when the kernel transport layer needs to locate a TCP (listening) or UDP (unconnected) socket for a new connection. Established TCP and UDP sockets do not trigger the BPF program.

There are two valid return codes for **BPF_PROG_TYPE_SK_LOOKUP** programs:

- **SK_DROP (0)**: Drop the connection
- **SK_PASS (1)**: Allow the connection to proceed either via normal processes or socket assignment using the **bpf_sk_assign()** helper.

BPF **sk_lookup** program can be attached to a network namespace using a BPF link to attach to a network namespace file descriptor. See **ch08/BPF_PROG_TYPE_SK_LOOKUP** in the GitHub repository for a full example.

Socket lookup programs need to find a socket from the **socket_map** map to assign the incoming connection to an existing serving socket.

In this example, we have two maps, one **port_map** which tracks the ports that the BPF program should be listening to and assigning ports to. The second map is a socket map that maps a port number to a socket ready to serve the incoming connection:

```
SEC("sk_lookup")
int echo_dispatch(struct bpf_sk_lookup *ctx) {
    __u16 port = ctx->local_port;
    bpf_printk("New connection for: %i\n", port);
    __u8 *open = bpf_map_lookup_elem(&port_map, &port);
    if (!open)
        return SK_PASS;

    const __u32 key     = 0;
     struct bpf_sock *sk = bpf_map_lookup_elem(&socket_map,
&key);
    if (!sk)
        return SK_DROP;

    long err = bpf_sk_assign(ctx, sk, 0);
    bpf_sk_release(sk);
    return err ? SK_DROP : SK_PASS;
}
```

See **ch08/BPF_PROG_TYPE_SK_LOOKUP** in the GitHub repository for a full example.

We recommend the following supporting resources:

- **https://docs.kernel.org/bpf/prog_sk_lookup.html**

- **https://arthurchiao.art/blog/pidfd-and-socket-lookup-bpf-illustrated/**

- **https://lwn.net/Articles/819618/**

- **https://blog.cloudflare.com/tubular-fixing-the-socket-api-with-ebpf/**

- **https://ebpf.io/summit-2020-slides/eBPF_Summit_2020-Lightning-Jakub_Sitnicki-Steering_connections_to_sockets_with_BPF_socke_lookup_hook.pdf**

- **https://www.micahlerner.com/2022/01/13/the-ties-that-un-bind-decoupling-ip-from-web-services-and-sockets-for-robust-addressing-agility-at-cdn-scale.html**

Netfilter programs

Netfilter is the newest BPF program type that allows you to execute eBPF programs in **nftables** hooks. When a packet enters or leaves a network interface, it goes through a series of processing steps in **nftables**, and hooks allow you to attach filtering rules (in this case, BPF programs) at specific points in this processing flow. These hooks determine when a set of rules should be applied to packets. The following are the attributes of the program type:

Program type name	BPF_PROG_TYPE_NETFILTER
Kernel version introduced	6.4
BPF program context	`struct bpf_nf_ctx`
BPF attachment types	`BPF_LINK_TYPE_NETFILTER`
ELF sections	`netfilter`

Table 8.17: BPF_PROG_TYPE_NETFILTER properties

When you create filtering rules in nftables, you specify the hook at which the rule should be applied. For example, if you want to filter incoming packets targeting a specific port, you would typically create a rule in the input hook. Similarly, if you want to perform **Network Address Translation (NAT)** on outgoing packets, you would create rules in the postrouting hook. The following a list of available netfilter hooks:

- **Prerouting**: This hook is triggered when a packet enters the network stack before any routing decisions are made. It is useful for performing actions on packets before they are routed to their destination.

- **Input**: Packets are destined for the local system trigger this hook. Filtering rules in the input hook are typically used to control packets targeted at the local machine.

- **Forward**: This hook is triggered when packets are being forwarded from one network interface to another within the system. It is used for filtering packets that are passing through the system but not destined for it.

- **Output**: Packets generated by the local system, such as responses to incoming requests, trigger this hook. Filtering rules in the output hook control the packets originating from the local machine.

- **Postrouting**: This hook is triggered after routing decisions have been made and just before the packet leaves the system. It is used for performing actions on packets before they leave the network stack.

BPF_PROG_TYPE_NETFILTER programs return one of the following two options which represent how the packet should be processed:

- **NF_DROP (0)**: Drop the packet.

- **NF_ACCEPT (1)**: Accept the packet.

To attach a BPF program, you will need to create a netfilter link. Take a look at the following code:

```
union bpf_attr attr = { };
attr.link_create.prog_fd = progfd;
attr.link_create.attach_type = 0; /* unused */
attr.link_create.netfilter.pf = PF_INET;
attr.link_create.netfilter.hooknum = NF_INET_LOCAL_IN;
attr.link_create.netfilter.priority = -128;
err = bpf(BPF_LINK_CREATE, &attr, sizeof(attr));
```

Note: Priorities must be unique in any given hook type.

The **bpf_nf_ctx** gives you access to a **skb** in which you can write conditional packet parsing statements with:

```
SEC("netfilter")
int nf_test(struct bpf_nf_ctx *ctx)
{
    struct __sk_buff *skb = (struct __sk_buff *)ctx->skb;
    const struct nf_hook_state *state = ctx->state;
    const struct iphdr *iph;
    const struct tcphdr *th;
    u8 buffer_iph[20] = {};
    u8 buffer_th[40] = {};
    struct bpf_dynptr ptr;
    uint8_t ihl;

    if (ctx->skb->len <= 20 || bpf_dynptr_from_skb(skb, 0, &ptr))
        return NF_ACCEPT;
    iph = bpf_dynptr_slice(&ptr, 0, buffer_iph,
```

```
sizeof(buffer_iph));
    if (!iph)
        return NF_ACCEPT;
    if (state->pf != 2)
        return NF_ACCEPT;
    ihl = iph->ihl << 2;
    th = bpf_dynptr_slice(&ptr, ihl, buffer_th,
sizeof(buffer_th));
    if (!th)
        return NF_ACCEPT;
    return th->dest == bpf_htons(80) ? NF_DROP : NF_ACCEPT;
}
```

We recommend the following supporting resources:

- **https://wiki.nftables.org/wiki-nftables/index.php/Netfilter_
hooks**

Conclusion

As you can see by the variety of network program types that cover the whole, eBPF provides significant functional flexibility in many areas of Linux networking. eBPF networking programs have been transformational at companies like Facebook and Cloudflare. When thinking about writing network eBPF programs, consider your objectives and which program type best suits your cause.

In the next chapter, eBPF security, we will review how you can use eBPF to implement detective and preventative security controls. This will cover simple concepts from firewalls to sysctl tampering and **Linux Security Module (LSM)** integrations.

Join our book's Discord space

Join the book's Discord Workspace for Latest updates, Offers, Tech happenings around the world, New Release and Sessions with the Authors:

https://discord.bpbonline.com

CHAPTER 9
eBPF Security

Introduction

While eBPF provides a number of options that could be used in a security context, security is often not at the forefront of the discussion of eBPF programming. Given eBPF's unique (and holistic) ability to view nearly any kernel interaction, it makes sense to use eBPF for security purposes.

Several eBPF program types are provided for dedicated security purposes (monitoring and enforcement). There are a number of eBPF security projects that we will discuss at the end of this chapter.

Structure

In this chapter, we will cover the following topics:

- Introduction to security observability
- eBPF security program types
- cgroup device controls
- Monitoring cgroup sysctl controls

- Firewalls for container networks
- BPF for Linux Security Modules
- Open source eBPF security projects

Objectives

In this chapter, we aim to introduce four new eBPF program types that can be used to provide security controls in cgroups and host systems. You will learn how to use these programs to build preventative and monitoring controls.

Introduction to eBPF security tooling

Security monitoring consists of passive observability (with a security focus) and active analysis of network activity (known as **monitoring controls**). The following figure by *Brendan Gregg* illustrates areas that you could monitor passively for suspicious behavior. Many of these fall under observability, which was covered in *Chapter 3, eBPF Programming Concepts*.

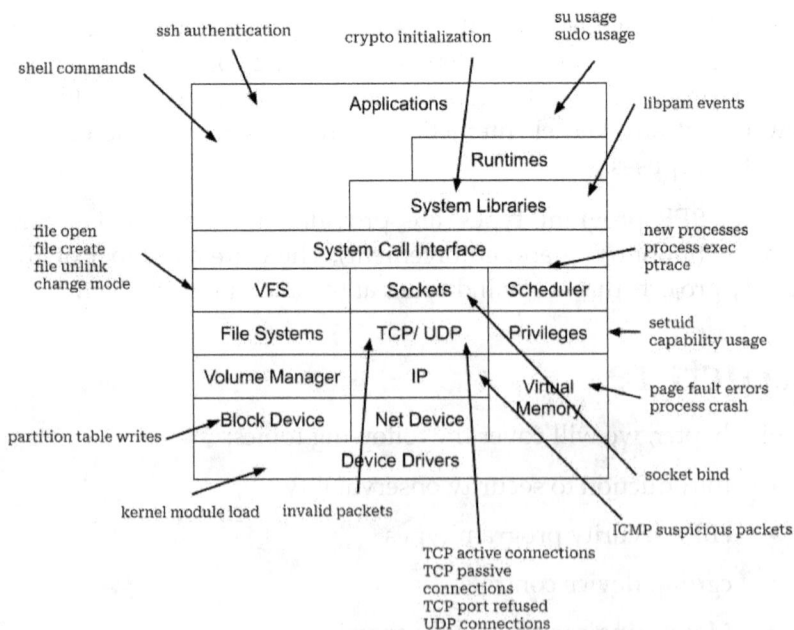

Figure 9.1: What to monitor

The key areas to highlight are:

- Newly created processes
- Privilege escalation
- Capability usage

Good security monitoring has low-level access to the kernel and can passively detect a high rate of events with minimal performance impact. These characteristics play to eBPF's strengths as an ecosystem.

You should reach *Brendan's* blog post that warns against the use of the current BCC tools for security purposes. Any critical security controls (either monitoring or preventative), should be implemented using **Linux Security Modules** (**LSM**) BPF programs (more on these later in the chapter).

eBPF security program types

eBPF provides three more security-minded program-types that can be used as active security measures. These are:

- **BPF_PROG_TYPE_CGROUP_DEVICE**: Control a cgroup's access to host devices.

- **BPF_PROG_TYPE_CGROUP_SYSCTL**: Control/monitor a cgroup's access to host sysctl's.

- **BPF_PROG_TYPE_CGROUP_SKB**: Control network ingress/egress to a cgroup similar to **BPF_PROG_TYPE_SOCKET_FILTER**.

- **BPF_PROG_TYPE_LSM**: Allow runtime instrumentation of the LSM hooks to implement system-wide **mandatory access control** (**MAC**) and audit policies using eBPF.

We will now explain each program type in detail.

cgroup device controls

cgroupsv1 contained a device controller that allows an administrator (root user) to limit what devices a cgroup (container) could access (both read and write). The cgroupsV2 does not contain a device controller, so in its absence, a **BPF_PROG_TYPE_CGROUP_DEVICE** program can be used to provide similar functionality with some extra flexibility.

Program Type Name	BPF_PROG_TYPE_CGROUP_DEVICE
Kernel version introduced	4.15
BPF program context	**struct bpf_cgroup_dev_ctx**
BPF Attachment types	BPF_CGROUP_DEVICE
ELF sections	**cgroup/dev**

Table 9.1: BPF_PROG_TYPE_CGROUP_DEVICE program attributes

The **BPF_PROG_TYPE_CGROUP_DEVICE** program type takes a major and minor device number, a device type (block/character), and access type (mknod/read/write) as parameters and returns an integer that defines if the operator should be allowed or terminated with **EPERM** (operation not permitted).

The program context struct takes three arguments:

- The **access_type** encodes the type of device (for example, block or char) and the permission it wants (read, write, mknod).

- The **major** and **minor** represent the programmatic way to access (address) a certain device. You can find more about device numbers on the kernel documentation page (**https://www.kernel.org/doc/Documentation/admin-guide/devices.txt**). You can find the major and minor versions of devices available on your system by running: **udevadm info --export-db**.

The use is straightforward. The BPF kernel-space program is fed the context **bpf_cgroup_dev_ctx** which provides information about the type of the device (block or character), type of access (read/write), and the major/minor numbers of the device.

In the following example program, we create a basic filter to only allow devices 0:5 (**/dev/zero**) and 0:9 (**/dev/urandom**) to be accessed. Any attempt to access any other devices will be denied:

```
int bpf_prog1(struct bpf_cgroup_dev_ctx *ctx){
    short type = ctx->access_type & 0xFFFF;
    short access = ctx->access_type >> 16;
    char fmt[] = "Access to device: %d:%d attempted\n";
    bpf_trace_printk(fmt, sizeof(fmt), ctx->major, ctx->minor);

    if (type != BPF_DEVCG_DEV_CHAR) {
```

```
        char fmt3[] = "Not a character device";
        bpf_trace_printk(fmt3, sizeof(fmt3));
        return 0;
    }

    /* Ensure major number is 1 (Character devices: zero,
urandom, null, etc.) */
    if (ctx->major != 1) {
        return 0; // Deny if not major 1
    }

    /* Allow only specific minor numbers */
    if (ctx->minor == 3 || ctx->minor == 5 || ctx->minor
== 9) {
        return 1; // Allow /dev/null (1:3), /dev/zero
(1:5) and /dev/urandom (1:9)
    }
    return 0; // Deny everything else
}
```

We recommend the following supporting resources:

- https://dropbear.xyz/2023/05/23/devices-with-cgroup-v2/
- https://docs.kernel.org/admin-guide/cgroup-v2.html#device-controller

Monitoring cgroup sysctl controls

Some containerized applications may run as root, which can potentially cause programs for the underlying host. Specifically, in this case, an application may be able to change a sysctl and adversely affect other applications running on the host. The **BPF_PROG_TYPE_CGROUP_SYSCTL** program type provides access control mechanisms to sysctl.

Program type name	BPF_PROG_TYPE_CGROUP_SYSCTL
Kernel version introduced	5.2
BPF program context	**struct bpf_sysctl**
BPF Attachment types	BPF_CGROUP_SYSCTL
ELF sections	**cgroup/sysctl**

Table 9.2: BPF_PROG_TYPE_CGROUP_SYSCTL program attributes

Depending on your infrastructure, you may not be able to block the ability to disable writing to sysctl. The **BPF_PROG_TYPE_CGROUP_SYSCTL** program type is intended to be attached to a cgroup and will be called every time a process inside that cgroup tries to read from or write to a sysctl setting.

The following context is parsed into the BPF program:

```
struct bpf_sysctl {
    __u32 write;
    __u32 file_pos;
};
```

The **write** element indicates whether the value of the sysctl is being read (0) or written (1). This field is read-only.

The **file_pos** indicates the file position that sysctl is being accessed at (read or written). This field is read-write:

- Writing a non-zero value to the field is used to set the starting position where the value is being read from or written to.

- Writing zero to the field allows you to use the BPF helper **bpf_sysctl_set_new_value()** to override the value provided from user-space.

- Not all sysctl allow **file_pos** to be set as a non-zero value. For example, writes to numeric sysctl entries must always be at file position 0.

If a kernel-space BPF program returns 0, user space will get -1 from **read(2)** or **write(2),** and error number will be set to **EPERM**. If the BPF program returns 1, user-space can proceed with the action.

We will now demonstrate an example program that runs when an access attempt is made to the **net/ipv4/ip_forward** sysctl. If it is a write request, the request is denied except for **net/ipv4/ip_forward**. All read requests will be allowed.

```
static __always_inline int is_ip_forwarding(struct bpf_sysctl *ctx)
{
    char name[64];
    int ret;
    memset(name, 0, sizeof(name));
    ret = bpf_sysctl_get_name(ctx, name, sizeof(name), 0);
```

```
    if (ret < 0)
        return 0;
    // Manually compare the bytes of the name to "net/
ipv4/ip_forward"
    char ip_forwarding_name[] = "net/ipv4/ip_forward";
    for (int i = 0; i < sizeof(ip_forwarding_name) - 1;
++i) {
        if (name[i] != ip_forwarding_name[i])
            return 0;
    }
    return 1;
}

SEC("cgroup/sysctl")
int sysctl_ip_forwarding(struct bpf_sysctl *ctx)
{
    if (ctx->write) {
        // Deny all writes except for "net/ipv4/ip_forward"
        if (is_ip_forwarding(ctx))
            return 1;  // Allow the write access to "net/
ipv4/ip_forward"
    } else {
        // Allow all reads
        return 1;
    }
    return 0;  // Deny all other sysctl operations
}
```

BPF_PROG_TYPE_CGROUP_SYSCTL is intended to be used in a trusted root environment, to monitor sysctl usage or catch unreasonable values an application, running as root in a separate cgroup, is trying to set. You should not use this program type to limit sysctl actions by specific processes or cgroups. You can read more as to why this is in the kernel documentation (see below).

You find more about **BPF_PROG_TYPE_CGROUP_SYSCTL** in these articles:

- **https://docs.kernel.org/bpf/prog_cgroup_sysctl.html**

- **https://lwn.net/Articles/785263/**

Firewalls for container networks

The **BPF_PROG_TYPE_CGROUP_SKB** program behaves similarly to **BPF_PROG_TYPE_SOCKET_FILTER**, but the difference is that this program type only works within the given cgroup. This allows the filtering of traffic incoming to the cgroup before being delivered to a process. The behavior of the **BPF_PROG_TYPE_CGROUP_SKB** filter applies to all processes within the filter (which creates immense flexibility).

Program type name	BPF_PROG_TYPE_CGROUP_SKB
Kernel version introduced	4.10
BPF program context	**struct __sk_buff**
BPF Attachment types	BPF_CGROUP_INET_EGRESS BPF_CGROUP_INET_INGRESS
ELF sections	**cgroup/skb** **cgroup_skb/egress** **cgroup_skb/ingress**

Table 9.3: BPF_PROG_TYPE_CGROUP_SKB program attributes

The **BPF_PROG_TYPE_CGROUP_SKB** program is attached to the cgroup's file descriptor. BPF programs should return 1 to allow access. Any other value results in the function **cgroup_bpf_run_filter_skb()** returning -**EPERM**, which will be propagated to the caller such that the packet is dropped.

Given how much time we have spent on socket filters in *Chapter 8, eBPF Networking,* we will write a simple BPF program here that will drop all incoming packets to the attached cgroup:

```
SEC("cgroup/skb")
int skb_filter(struct __sk_buff *skb) {
    //drop all traffic
    return 0;
}
```

Recommended reading:

https://lwn.net/Articles/698073/https://aya-rs.dev/book/programs/cgroup-skb/https://nfil.dev/coding/security/ebpf-firewall-with-cgroups/

BPF for Linux Security Modules

LSM is the framework integrated into the kernel to provide the necessary components to implement the MAC modules without having the need to change the kernel source code every time.

Program type name	BPF_PROG_TYPE_LSM
Kernel version introduced	5.7
BPF program context	Dependent on the hook. See more below
BPF Attachment types	BPF_LSM_CGROUP BPF_LSM_MAC
ELF sections	`lsm[.s]/<hook>` `lsm_cgroup/<hook>`

Table 9.4: BPF_PROG_TYPE_LSM program attributes

The LSM framework is intended to allow security modules to lock down a system by inserting checks whenever the kernel is about to perform an action regarding the following concepts:

- Files

- Sockets and tunnels

- Inodes

- task structures

- Credentials and capabilities

- **Inter-process communication (IPC)** objects.

There is a partial list of current LSM hooks that are available in the kernel documentation (**https://www.kernel.org/doc/html/latest/security/lsm-development.html**). You can find a full list of hooks in `include/linux/lsm_hook_defs.h`. Look for function names that start with **LSM_HOOK** (You should also take note of the arguments for each hook, as these will be needed for your BPF program context).

An LSM hook is defined in the following way:

```
LSM_HOOK(
    Int,        // Return Type
    0,          // Default Return Value
    bprm_check_security,  //Name of hook
    struct linux_binprm * bprm    // Parameters of hook
```

LSM hooks are a secure way to perform auditing and mandatory access control and are a more secure way of providing both preventative and monitoring security controls. You should double-check that your system supports BPF LSM by running:

```
$ cat /sys/kernel/security/lsm
capability,lockdown,landlock,yama,apparmor,bpf
```

You should see **bpf** in the output. If you do not, you'll need to reconfigure your kernel to include this option.

We will write an example security control that denies any process from being able to open any file that is within the **/tmp** directory:

```
#define EPERM 1

SEC("lsm/file_open")
int BPF_PROG(restrict_tmp_file_open, struct file *file)
{
    char path[256];
    struct dentry *dentry = file->f_path.dentry;
    struct vfsmount *mnt = file->f_path.mnt;

    /* Get the full file path */
    if (bpf_d_path(&file->f_path, path, sizeof(path)) < 0)
        return 1;   /* Fail closed if path retrieval fails */

    /* Check if the file is in /tmp */
    if (__builtin_memcmp(path, "/tmp", 4) == 0) {
        bpf_printk("LSM: Blocking file open in /tmp: %s\n", path);
        return -EPERM;
    }
    return 0;
}
```

While it is useful to write preventive BPF LSM programs that block actions, it is equally as useful as a way to perform auditing against highly sensitive systems. Do remember that these programs may be executed frequently, so ensure that they optimized in a way that makes sense for your environment.

You can learn more about LSM and **BPF_PROG_TYPE_LSM** programs from the following resources:

https://elinux.org/images/0/0a/ELC_Inside_LSM.pdf

https://www.accuknox.com/blog/an-introduction-to-linux-security-modules

https://www.kernel.org/doc/html/latest/security/lsm.html

https://lwn.net/Articles/813057/

https://aya-rs.dev/book/programs/lsm/#what-is-lsm

Open source eBPF security projects

The desire for highly configurable security enforcement tools has led to several projects becoming popular and being used for their security observability functions:

1. **Falco**: Falco (**https://sysdig.com/opensource/falco/**) is one of the most well-known projects in the *Cloud Native Computing Foundation* (*CNCF*) landscape. It uses eBPF to perform runtime intrusion detection on containers and their host systems.

2. **Tetragon**: Tetragon (**https://github.com/cilium/tetragon**) is an open-source project created by Cilium that performs a wide range of runtime checks of application behavior using eBPF programs. It does provide real-time enforcement of preconfigured rules.

3. **Suricata-EBPF and eBPF-based Snort**: Suricata (**https://docs.suricata.io/en/latest/capture-hardware/ebpf-xdp.html**) and Snort have been around for years and are well known by those in the security space. They have been updated to support XDP bypass which allows for higher throughput monitoring.

4. **Pulsar**: Pulsar (**https://pulsar.sh/docs/**) is a Rust based eBPF security observability framework. It contains a rules engine that lets you configure specific detections to alert on. It can primarily monitor four systems of activity: file I/O, network traffic, processes, and system activity (device activity and system calls).

Conclusion

eBPF offers new features that enable low-level security observability and defensive enforcement measures that will ultimately enhance the security landscape.

As the eBPF framework and its features continue to evolve, the way container, network, monitoring, and security applications are written will continue to move toward eBPF. The high-performance, low-level, and (kernel) safety features that eBPF embodies make it a platform to build the next wave of Linux system applications.

Join our book's Discord space

Join the book's Discord Workspace for Latest updates, Offers, Tech happenings around the world, New Release and Sessions with the Authors:

https://discord.bpbonline.com

# CHAPTER 10

eBPF Open Source Projects and the Future of eBPF

Introduction

This book has gone into great detail on the origins of eBPF and the features and functionality that is currently available. This final chapter will reflect on the projects and frameworks that have contributed to making eBPF a very successful technology. It will also look forward to the future and explain the new features and governance that will come to the ecosystem.

Structure

In this chapter, we will cover the following topics:

- Introduction to the eBPF open source landscape
- Language projects
- Notable open source projects
- The future of eBPF

Objectives

By the end of this chapter, you will be familiar with some of the most popular eBPF projects and their uses, as well as the most popular language frameworks. Finally, you will learn what is coming to the eBPF ecosystem in the near future.

Introduction to eBPF's open source projects

eBPFs usefulness has exponentially grown over the past ten years. It has gone from a simple packet filter to one of the most exciting features of the Linux kernel. Probably most importantly, it has made kernel module development essentially obsolete.

eBPF has enabled some very successful companies to build revolutionary products; Isovalent, Flowmil, and Pixie Labs, to name a few. Over the last decade, however, there has been a wide array of successful open-source eBPF-based projects that have propelled the ecosystem forward.

While the aforementioned companies have brought eBPF technology to the enterprise, there's no question that open-source projects like the BCC have made eBPF easily accessible to the masses.

Language projects

As we covered in *Chapter 4, eBPF Programming Libraries and Frameworks*, there are a large number of open source projects that allow you to run user-space eBPF programs with the accompanying C in-kernel counterparts. In this section, we will briefly list all of the relevant language projects in the eBPF ecosystem:

- **C**: While the bar for entry to purely use the C platform is high, it is a popular way to build eBPF kernel and user-space programs. These are the most prominent libraries:
  - o **libbpf (https://github.com/libbpf/libbpf)**: libbpf is the go to library in the eBPF space to load and run BPF programs.
  - o **Iovisor/bcc (https://github.com/iovisor/bcc/)**: While BCC is best known for its Python bindings, it also supports C.

- o **trailofbits/ebpf-common (https://github.com/ trailofbits/ebpfpub/)**: It is a library that allows you to write tracing programs in C++.

- **Go**: Golang has a number of libraries that are available for use, including:

  - o **iovisor/gobpf (https://github.com/iovisor/gobpf)**: goebpf is a Go equivalent library for BCC framework.

  - o **cilium/ebpf (https://github.com/cilium/ebpf)**: ebpf-go is a pure Go based library from Cilium / Isovalent.

  - o **aquasecurity/libbpfgo (https://github.com/ aquasecurity/libbpfgo)**: It is a thin Go wrapper around libbpf that allows you to have all the benefits of BTF and CO-RE in Go.

  - o **dropbox/goebpf (https://github.com/dropbox/goebpf)**: It is the basic Go library that allows you to load and run socket filter, XDP, Kprobe, TC, and perf programs.

- **Python**: Python has the lowest barrier to entry and there is a plethora of examples available to start your eBPF programming journey. None of them support CO-RE at this time. Here is a list of the largest eBPF Python language projects:

  - o **iovisor/bcc (https://github.com/iovisor/bcc)**: As we have largely covered in this book, BCC is the standard Python framework to use.

  - o **dany74q/pyebpf (https://github.com/dany74q/pyebpf)**: This library wraps BCC but will also translate your kernel-space code from Python into C for you (saving you from writing C code).

- **Rust**: Rust has three prominent libraries that provide good compatible eBPF portability features:

  - o **redcanaryco/oxidebpf (https://github.com/ redcanaryco/oxidebpf)**: It is a CO-RE-supported pure Rust eBPF library.

  - o **aya-rs/aya (https://github.com/aya-rs/aya)**: It is a BTF-supported library built purely in Rust.

  - o **libbpf/libbpf-rs (https://github.com/libbpf/libbpf-rs)**: It is a simple Rust wrapper around libbpf.

- **WASM**: Finally, while the WebAssembly ecosystem is relatively new, there is a mature project to run eBPF in WebAssembly:

  - **eunomia-bpf (https://github.com/eunomia-bpf/ eunomia-bpf)**: It is a compilation framework and runtime library to build, distribute, dynamically load, and run CO-RE eBPF applications in WebAssembly. It allows you to be CO-RE supported eBPF or with. The library supports writing eBPF kernel code only (to build simple CO-RE libbpf eBPF applications), writing the kernel part in C, and writing user-space in multiple languages in a WASM module and distributing it with simple JSON data or WASM OCI images.

Notable open source projects

It would be remiss to not highlight the open source projects that are either built from eBPF or utilize eBPF extensively. We will look at these projects through the lens of observability, networking, and security.

Observability

Given that many of the early features in eBPF revolved around observability applications, it is unsurprising that there are a significant number of open-source observability projects. Here is a list of the most prominent projects: bpftrace (**https://github.com/iovisor/bpftrace**): bpftrace is an easy-to-use tracing scripting language based on the BCC library that allows you to create one-line tracing commands with kprobes, uprobes, and tracepoints:

- **Pixie (https://docs.px.dev/about-pixie/pixie-ebpf/)**: Pixie is an open-source observability tool for Kubernetes applications. It uses eBPF to capture telemetry data without the need for manual instrumentation.

- **SkyWalking Rover (https://skywalking.apache.org/docs/ main/next/en/setup/backend/backend-ebpf-profiling/)**: Apache SkyWalking is an open-source observability platform used to collect, analyze, aggregate and visualize data from services and cloud native infrastructures.

You can find a larger list of observability projects in the awesome-ebpf repository (**https://github.com/zoidyzoidzoid/awesome-ebpf**).

Networking

As we have covered at length, eBPF has a plethora of networking use cases. You will see many of these captured in the following projects:

- **Cilium (https://github.com/cilium/cilium)**: It is probably the best-known piece of eBPF software. Cilium provides software deployed with Docker and Kubernetes and provides functionality that is powered by eBPF program types, such as:TC and XDP,

- **Katran (https://github.com/facebookincubator/katran)**: *Facebook* wrote Katran, an XDP-based L4 load balancer. It distributes all incoming traffic to its edge servers at all of its edge-pop locations.

- **Calico (https://docs.tigera.io/calico/latest/operations/ebpf/ enabling-ebpf)**: Calico is a popular Kubernetes **Container Network Interface** (**CNI**) that allows you to perform data encryption, IPAM management, network policy enforcement, and implement overlay networks.

- **Hubble (https://github.com/cilium/hubble)**: Hubble is a network and security observability platform from the Cilium project. It provides layer-7 network visibility into network traffic, which gives you full visibility of all Kubernetes traffic.

Security

The desire for low-level, highly configurable security enforcement tools has led to a number of eBPF projects becoming popular and being used for their security observability functions, including:

- **Falco (https://sysdig.com/opensource/falco/)**: Falco is one of the most well-known projects in the CNCF landscape. Falco uses eBPF to perform runtime intrusion detection on containers and their host systems.

- **Tetragon (https://github.com/cilium/tetragon)**: Tetragon is an open-source project created by Cilium that performs a wide range of runtime checks of application behavior using eBPF programs. It does provide real-time enforcement of preconfigured rules.

- **Suricata-EBPF (https://docs.suricata.io/en/latest/capture-hardware/ebpf-xdp.html)_and eBPF-based Snort**: Suricata and Snort have been around for years and are well known by those in the security space. They both have been updated to support XDP bypass which allows for higher throughput monitoring.

- **Pulsar (https://pulsar.sh/docs/)**: Pulsar is a Rust-based eBPF security observability framework. It contains a rules engine that lets you configure specific detections to alert on. It can primarily monitor four systems of activity: file I/O, network traffic, processes, and system activity (device activity and system calls).

The future of eBPF

eBPF has come a long way in the ten years since Alexei's initial commits. As technology continues to grow, efforts are being made to grow the community and standardize the technology.

For example, at the *2022 Linux Plumbers Conference*, eBPF maintainer *Alexei Starovoitov* gave a talk discussing how he expects to see the C language used by eBPF programs evolve. We have already seen eBPF evolve from supporting a few thousand instructions to practically unlimited complexity, with the addition of support for loops and an ever-increasing set of BPF helper functions. As additional capabilities are added into the C that is supported, and with the support of the verifier, eBPF C could evolve to allow all the flexibility of developing kernel modules, but with the safety and dynamic loading characteristics of eBPF.

Some of the other ideas being discussed and developed for new eBPF features and capabilities are covered in the next section.

eBPF foundation

In 2021, The Linux Foundation announced the creation of the *eBPF Foundation* (**https://ebpf.foundation**). The eBPF foundation's charter is to support open source eBPF projects and open standards related to eBPF technologies. Membership is currently only for companies that sponsor the foundation.

Standardization (IETF)

In 2022, at the LSFMM/ BPF conference, *Christoph Hellwig* proposed that the BPF ecosystem have formal specifications and thus be standardized. In the following months, an IETF BPF working group known as **BPF/eBPF (bpf)** was created.

The charter of the working group is to document the eBPF ecosystem and create both proposed standards and informational documents on the following items:

- **Proposed standards**
  - BPF **instruction set architecture (ISA)**
  - **BPF Type Format (BTF)**
  - Cross-platform map types
  - Cross-platform helper functions
  - Cross-platform BPF program types
- **Informational documents**
  - Verifier expectations
  - Conventions and guidelines
  - Producing portable BPF program binaries
  - Architecture and framework document.

The first RFC proposal is for eBPF ISA (**https://datatracker.ietf.org/doc/draft-ietf-bpf-isa/**).

You can find out more about the BPF standardization effort from the following resources:

- **Standardizing BPF: https://lwn.net/Articles/926882/**
- **BPF documentation and standardization**: **https://www.youtube.com/watch?v=9NmDqjfMKfo**
- **BPF/eBPF (bpf) IETF working group: https://datatracker.ietf.org/wg/bpf/about/**

Signing programs

BPF programs have effectively replaced the purpose of kernel modules (i.e., pluggable pieces of code that run in the kernel space). Kernel modules have the ability to be signed and verified before loading the module into the kernel.

At this time, eBPF does not have a fully functional signing and validation mechanism. *Alexei Starovoitov* introduced the **BPF_PROG_ TYPE_SYSCALL** program type as a first step towards introducing signed programs. However, the kernel cannot verify and enforce the map configuration intended by the program author, so there is no way to create fully signed eBPF programs currently.

BPF firewalls

Iptables came to Linux in version 2.4 in 2001, and its successor, nftables, was introduced in 3.13 in 2014, which allowed for an in-kernel virtual machine to implement firewall rules. In kernel 4.10, the ability to add BPF socket filter programs to iptables rules was introduced. This allows for complex BPF socket filters to analyze packets before allowing them to pass or be dropped.

This allows you to build BPF-based firewall rules, for example:

```
#include <linux/bpf.h>

int drop_from_192_168_1_100(struct sk_buff *skb) {
  // Get the source IP address of the packet.
  struct iphdr *iph = ip_hdr(skb);

  // If the source IP address is 192.168.1.100, drop the
packet.
  if (iph->saddr == 0xc0a80164) {
    return XDP_DROP;
  }

  // Otherwise, allow the packet to pass.
  return XDP_PASS;
}
```

It is then compiled and loaded into iptables as:

```
$ iptables -I INPUT -p tcp -j BPF --bytecode drop_
from_192.168.1.100.elf
```

Bpffilter was added to kernel 4.18 as a kernel module which is intended to be successor to iptables and nftables. While there has been little attention given to the work over the past five years, work has continued on the bpfilter project which takes traditional iptables rules and converts them into BPF filters.

As this article (**https://www.phoronix.com/news/BPFILTER-2021**) details, the performance numbers for bpfilter are impressive and are sure to generate interest, particularly for those who do not want to write their own XDP programs for high-performance firewalling.

eBPF security

In the past couple of years, a number of CVEs have been found in the eBPF kernel ecosystem, which has created some hesitancy around eBPF adoption, especially given eBPF's tight integration with kernel space. Further work has been done on the verifier and the basic structures around eBPF to build further safeguards to defend against general exploits in the use of eBPF.

Given eBPFs ability to interact directly with the kernel, it has become a popular tool for malware authors. Bpfdoor and Symbiote are known eBPF based Malware's in the wild. Red Canary has provided a detailed writeup (**https://redcanary.com/blog/threat-detection/ebpf-malware/**) of the current eBPF Malware landscape and some of the possible ways to detect and mitigate attacks. The bad BPF repo (**https://github.com/pathtofile/bad-bpf**) provides some great reference material on how eBPF can be used maliciously.

eBPF on Windows

As we covered briefly in *Chapter 4, eBPF Programming Libraries and Frameworks*, in 2021, *Microsoft* announced it was creating eBPF for Windows. This allows you to hook particular Windows kernel functions and use eBPF to create hardware drivers. It is important to note that eBPF for Windows is not a fork of Linux eBPF, but it does mimic a number of its paradigms.

There are currently five program types, including support for **XDP**, **SOCK_OPS**, and **CGROUP_SOCK_ADDR** programs, and 13 different map types. Microsoft Documentation provides more information about the supported BPF structures.

eBPF for Windows is supported on Windows 10 (and newer) as well as Windows Server 2019 (and newer). Importantly, Microsoft has leveraged the open source IOVisor uBPF project and the PREVAIL verifier projects to create the Windows based ecosystem.

Conclusion

Over the past ten years, BPF has undergone a massive transformation to become one of the most exciting technologies in the software industry. Technology has redefined how we observe systems, perform on-host networking functions, and provide new ways to secure systems. Throughout this book, we have explored the concept of eBPF, uncovering its powerful capabilities and the myriad ways it can be used.

As we conclude this book, it is important to recognize that the eBPF ecosystem is a dynamic and evolving landscape. New innovations, tools, and techniques will continue to emerge in each kernel version, further expanding the ways this technology can be used. The community around eBPF is vibrant and ever-growing, ensuring its potential will continue to be harnessed in increasingly creative and powerful ways.

Given the dynamic of the ecosystem, we recommend the following resources to keep up to date with the following resources:

- LWN (use the BPF tag): **https://lwn.net/Kernel/Index/#BPF**

- Kernel Newbies releases: **https://kernelnewbies.org/ LinuxChanges**

- eBPF weekly newsletter: **https://ebpf.io/newsletter/**

Thank you for taking the time to read this book. I sincerely hope that it has been a useful read to begin your immersion into the eBPF ecosystem. While new features will be added to eBPF for the foreseeable future, I hope this book will be a useful reference for years to come.

Join our book's Discord space

Join the book's Discord Workspace for Latest updates, Offers, Tech happenings around the world, New Release and Sessions with the Authors:

https://discord.bpbonline.com

Index

www.ingramcontent.com/pod-product-compliance
Lightning Source LLC
Chambersburg PA
CBHW061246220326
41599CB00028B/5551